An **IRISh COUNTRY** *Cookbook*

An Irish Country Cookbook

Patrick Taylor

WITH **DOROTHY TINMAN**

FORGE

A Tom Doherty Associates Book
New York

AN IRISH COUNTRY COOKBOOK

Copyright © 2017 by Ballybucklebo Stories Corp.

Photographs by John James Sherlock

Food styling by Antoinette Posehn and Darlene Sherlock

Illustrations by Rhys Davies

Designed by Greg Collins

A Forge Book
Published by Tom Doherty Associates
175 Fifth Avenue
New York, NY 10010

www.tor-forge.com

Forge® is a registered trademark of Macmillan Publishing Group, LLC.

The Library of Congress Cataloging-in-Publication Data is available upon request.

ISBN 978-0-7653-8278-8 (hardcover)
ISBN 978-0-7653-8279-5 (trade paperback)
ISBN 978-1-4668-8926-2 (e-book)

Our books may be purchased in bulk for promotional, educational, or business use. Please contact your local bookseller or the Macmillan Corporate and Premium Sales Department at 1-800-221-7945, extension 5442, or by e-mail at MacmillanSpecialMarkets@macmillan.com.

First Edition: February 2017

Printed in the United States of America

0   9   8   7   6   5   4   3   2   1

To Maureen and Joy

Contents

An IRISh COUNTRY Cookbook

Introduction

Hello there. Great oaks from little acorns grow and to everything there must be a start. Bear with me and I'll explain. My name is Barry Laverty; some of you may know me from reading Patrick Taylor's *Irish Country Doctor* series of books. If you do, you'll know a remarkable woman—Maureen "Kinky" Auchinleck, lately Kincaid, née O'Hanlon, housekeeper to the redoubtable Doctor Fingal Flahertie O'Reilly, physician and surgeon, and the font of all help to the folks who live in Ballybucklebo and the surrounding townland in County Down in Northern Ireland.

One Thursday afternoon in January 1967, after making home visits on one of Ulster's "let's pretend it's Monsoon season here" days, I barged through the back door into her kitchen at Number

One Main Street, rain dripping from my coat as if it were running off a spaniel after a water retrieve.

Kinky was sitting at her table writing something. She looked up. "Tut, Doctor Laverty," she said, shaking her head, "if it wasn't unfair to the animal in question I'd say you looked like a drowned rat, so. Did you swim home?"

I shrugged out of my coat. "No," I said, moving to stand in front of the range for a bit of warmth and rubbing my hands. "But there's a fellah in the back garden collecting up gopher wood and animals two by two. He says he's building an ark. Name's Noah."

She laughed. "Run away on with you, sir. But it surely does be coming down in sheets. Will I make you a cup of tea?"

"I think," I said, "you'll save a life. Mine."

She put what she was working on aside, rose, and set about tea making. "I wonder if I could ask you a favour, Doctor Laverty?"

Life was returning and my trouser legs were steaming. "Fire away."

She put a filled kettle on the range top. "You mind a few years back, himself, Doctor O'Reilly, asked me to give your man Patrick Taylor some traditional Irish recipes?"

"I do."

"And they were published in the back of all eleven of the *Irish Country* books? There's a fair wheen of them."

"Yes." I wondered where this was leading.

"Himself got to wondering aloud should I not put all that I know together in a book of my own?"

I had to grin. "I believe that would be a splendid idea, Kinky.

But what could I do for you? Sue Nolan says I'd burn water trying to boil an egg."

"Your fiancée is a very sensible woman but I'm not asking you to cook. I'm of the opinion," said Kinky, pouring boiling water into the teapot, "you could do me a very great service, so."

I frowned. "How?"

She emptied the pot, spooned in tea leaves, added more boiling water, and said, "We'll let that sit until it's well infused, then we'll both have a cup of tea and . . ." she went to a cupboard, "and a slice of my orange sponge cake, and I'll tell you what I have in mind. Sit you down, sir."

I did as I was told, wondering what Kinky could be thinking of.

In moments I was clutching a cuppa, munching on a slice of her exquisite orange sponge cake—Lord, but the woman could cook—and paying close attention to what she was saying.

"I think Doctor O'Reilly's right," she said, sitting opposite. "I do think I'd like to write a cookbook of my own and I do have some notions how to go about it, but I'd like your advice."

"I'll try," I said.

She indicated a fat folder on the tabletop. "There's at least 150 recipes in here, mine and some from my friends and an old, God rest her now, cook who used to work for the marquis." Kinky sat back and sipped her tea.

"That sounds like a pretty good start," I said.

"But," she said, "I'd like it to be more than just recipes. I'm already getting help from a Bangor woman called Dorothy Tinman. I met her when I took some art classes. She suggested I might like to include some signature recipes from a great Irish chef, and she's going to help me with all the conversions to North American and these newfangled metric measures and oven temperatures so anyone can use the book."

"Not me," I said, "but I do understand."

She glanced at my now-empty plate. "Another slice?"

"I shouldn't, but . . ." If, I thought, Kinky had been in charge of feeding up the fatted calf it would have been the size of a blue whale.

"Eat up however little much is in it," she said, putting a slice on my plate. "Now I do think that a lot of folks in America would like to see some pictures of Ireland. It is a very lovely country, so."

"I believe you're right. Pictures would add a lot," I said. The sponge just melted in my mouth.

"And Dorothy, who has a great soft hand under a duck when it comes to the oils, is willing to let me put in some of her paintings too."

"Sounds lovely," I said, having seen and much admired the artist's work in various art galleries in Belfast. "I'm sure recipes and illustrations would go down well. Now if seeking my advice was the favour, I hope I've done my duty. You go ahead, Kinky, and the best of luck."

"No, sir," she said. "I haven't quite finished."

I stopped a piece of cake halfway to my mouth. "What else could I possibly do?"

"Other than me, Doctor Laverty, no one, and I think that still might include his wife, Kitty, knows himself's practice and the people in it better than yourself."

I nodded.

"I'd like it very much if you'd have a stagger at putting pen to paper yourself and giving me a clatter of yarns about your first year here as his assistant that might bring a smile."

"Well I . . ."

"I know what it is you're going to say, sir, that you're no great shakes as a storyteller. You've always left that up to Patrick Taylor. I know for a fact he's banging away at his keyboard doing another *Country Doctor* book. I doubt if he'd have the time."

"I've heard," I said.

"So I have a plan."

"Go on," I said.

"My Da was one of the greatest *seanchies,* storytellers, in all of County Cork, and he passed on the gift to me."

I knew. I'd heard her. She was great.

"You just put them down through your own eyes, give them to me, and I'll give them a wee tweak. That's all it'll take. And sure if they do bring smiles to the readers' faces won't I be giving them more than just recipes?"

"Kinky," I said, "I think the idea is a good one, but I'm not sure I can pull it off."

She tutted and grabbed my cup. "Your tea's getting cold. I'll pour you a fresh cup." She trotted over to the sink, emptied the tea, came back, and repoured. "There," she said.

"Thank you."

"Now you'll give it a try, won't you, sir?"

And already I started to remember a famous occasion when

O'Reilly had lost his temper with two eminent professors—to their chagrin, not his. A certain lawyer who came to grief at O'Reilly's hands.

"Kinky," I said, "for you I'll give it a go."

"Grand altogether," she said, with a smile that would have chased the rain back to County Galway. "When can you give me the first?"

And that, dear reader, is how Kinky's cookbook got its start. It may not be a great oak like Isabella Beeton's *Book of Household Management*, but the recipes are all for very tasty grub, the pictures are lovely, and, Kinky says, the *craic* in the stories is ninety. We all hope you enjoy the reading of it and find the recipes fun to make and delicious to eat.

Beannacht De agat. God bless.

Barry Laverty

Dorothy Tinman

Kinky Auchinleck, lately Kincaid, née O'Hanlon

Explanation of Measurements

This book uses U.S. and metric measurements. In any recipe please use the same units throughout. Do not mix U.S. and metric.

All spoon measurements are level: a teaspoon is 5 ml and a tablespoon is 15 ml.

I have not used cups to measure because a cup of one ingredient will not necessarily measure the same as a cup of something else. It also depends on how tightly the cup is packed. Measuring by weight is more accurate than measuring by volume.

All eggs used are large.

All butter used is either salted or unsalted, unless otherwise noted. Where it would make a difference the type to be used will be specified. A knob of butter will be about a teaspoon and is usually the amount that it takes to grease a casserole or baking pan.

Individual vegetables, such as onions and potatoes, are assumed to be about 8 ounces or 227 grams.

However, here is a table of equivalent dry measurements for some common ingredients used in the recipes.

TABLE OF DRY MEASUREMENTS

	CUP	OZ	G
BREAD CRUMBS, DRY	1	4	113
BREAD CRUMBS, FRESH	1	1½	42.5
BUTTER, 1 STICK	½	4	113
CHEESE, GRATED, CHEDDAR	1	4	113
CHEESE, GRATED, PARMESAN	1	3½	100
FLOUR, ALL-PURPOSE	1	4½	127
FLOUR, SELF-RISING	1	4	113
FLOUR, WHOLE-WHEAT	1	4	113
OATS	1	3½	100
RICE, LONG-GRAIN, DRY	1	7	200
SUGAR, CONFECTIONERS'	1	4	113
SUGAR, DEMERARA	1	7¾	220
SUGAR, GRANULATED	1	7	200

LIQUID MEASUREMENTS

U.S. FLUID OUNCES	MILLILITERS
2	60
5	147
10	295
15	440
20	590

Temperature Chart

This chart shows the approximate temperatures between electric and gas ovens. You can see the conversions are really quite simple, as Celsius temperatures are approximately half of the Fahrenheit value. For fan-assisted and convection ovens, the temperature should be set a little lower and the cooking time reduced. Your manufacturer's handbook will give guidance on this.

Cooking times may vary according to the particular oven and are an approximate guide only.

FAHRENHEIT	CELSIUS	GAS MARK	DESCRIPTION
225	110	¼	extremely cool
250	130	½	very cool
275	140	1	cool
300	150	2	cool
325	170	3	very moderate
350	180	4	moderate
375	190	5	moderately hot
400	200	6	moderately hot
425	220	7	hot
450	230	8	hot
475	240	9	extremely hot

STARTERS

Soups

In the wintertime when Doctor O'Reilly was going duck shooting down to Strangford Lough, he liked to take a flask of soup with him, usually some hard-boiled or Scotch eggs, and a good chunk of bread and some cheddar cheese. He said that being out on a cold, frosty morning waiting for the dawn and the ducks of course gave him a great appetite. Sure isn't it grand but I never found his appetite to be anything but insatiable.

Real chicken stock is something that a reasonably good cook is likely to have at hand or in the freezer. If you boil a chicken to cook it then what you have left is real chicken stock. People also cook chicken carcasses to make stock.

However, stock cubes or powder are as good a substitute and make for a quick tasty soup.

This is one of his favourites:

Creamy Chicken Soup

Serves 4

1 Tbsp butter

1 Tbsp oil

1 medium, boneless chicken breast, diced, skin removed

1 large onion, chopped

1 large potato, peeled and chopped

20 oz/590 ml chicken stock (you can use stock cubes)

10 oz/295 ml milk

Salt and freshly ground black pepper

Heavy cream

Finely chopped fresh parsley

Melt the butter with the oil in a large saucepan and sauté the pieces of chicken, turning frequently to lightly brown them on all sides. Remove the chicken from the pan and set aside. Now add the onion and potato to the pan and stir gently over a very low heat to prevent sticking. Cover with a piece of parchment paper and the pan lid. Continue to sweat gently for about 10 minutes, stirring occasionally, until the onion is translucent and the potato has softened. Discard the parchment.

Return the chicken to the pan, add the stock, and bring back to the boil. Continue to simmer gently for about 30 minutes. Allow to cool slightly, add the milk, and season with salt and pepper. Liquidise the soup using an immersion blender or food processor. Serve with a little swirl of cream and some parsley.

Kinky's Note:

Covering the vegetables with parchment paper and cooking very gently creates steam and is called "sweating." This enables the maximum amount of moisture and flavour to be extracted.

Pea and Ham Soup

Serves 4 to 6

1 lb 2 oz/500 g dried peas

1 large onion, peeled

10 whole cloves

1 ham bone, plus 6 oz/170 g diced cooked ham

48 oz/1.4 L ham stock or vegetable stock cubes

2 or 3 bay leaves

Salt and freshly ground black pepper

Chopped fresh parsley

Heavy cream

Soak the peas overnight in cold water. The next day drain them and place them in a large saucepan. Stud the onion with the cloves and add it to the pan, along with the ham bone, stock, and bay leaves. Bring to the boil. As the peas come to the boil, a scum will come to the surface so just skim and discard this. Leave to boil for about an hour, by which time the peas should be soft.

Remove the bone, onion, and bay leaves and liquidise the remainder with a blender or food processor. Taste before seasoning with salt, as the ham stock may be quite salty. Add the freshly ground black pepper, diced ham, parsley, and a generous swirl of cream to the soup before serving.

Jerusalem Artichoke Soup
with Croutons

Jerusalem artichokes, also called sunchokes, are a much-neglected winter vegetable. They are very easy to grow, so easy in fact that if you are planning to try, just remember that they are also a very invasive plant. The tubers grow like potatoes underground and if you don't manage to dig them all up they will multiply and come back again with a vengeance the following season. They were introduced to Europe in the seventeenth century by the French explorer Samuel de Champlain, who discovered them growing in Cape Cod.

Jerusalem artichokes are a member of the sunflower family and, like their flower relations, also grow very tall. The name is thought to have been a corruption of the word *girasol* which means "sunflower" in Italian. They look like knobbly potatoes and are not easy to peel. However, if they are fresh and firm without too many knobs and bumps, you may only need to give them a good brushing in cold water to clean them.

Serves 6 to 8

2 oz/56 g butter

2¼ lb/1 kg Jerusalem artichokes, cleaned and chopped

1¼ lb/570 g potatoes, peeled and chopped

1¼ lb/570 g onions, chopped

Salt and freshly ground black pepper

40 oz/1.2 L chicken stock

20 oz/590 ml milk

Chopped fresh parsley

Croutons (recipe follows)

Sesame oil or maple syrup

Melt the butter in a large, heavy-bottomed saucepan, then add the artichokes, potatoes, and onions. Season with salt and pepper. Cover with parchment paper and the pan lid and sweat gently over a low heat for about 10 minutes, checking often to ensure that the vegetables are not sticking. Remove the parchment paper, add the stock, and cook for another 10 to 15 minutes until the vegetables are soft. Liquidise the soup using a blender, food processor, or immersion blender and return to the heat. Thin to the consistency of thick cream, adding the milk gradually, and season with salt and pepper to taste. Ladle into individual bowls, sprinkle with parsley and croutons, drizzle with oil or syrup, and serve.

Croutons
Butter 4 slices of thick white bread. Cut into cubes, spread onto a baking sheet, and bake in a 375°F/190°C oven for about 10 minutes until golden brown.

VARIATION
Parsnip and Apple Soup. Substitute peeled, chopped parsnips for the potatoes, and peeled, cored, and chopped tart apples for the artichokes. Drizzle with maple syrup instead of oil.

Kinky's Note:
Whilst Bramley apples would have been the cooking apples of choice in Ulster, if they are not available, try using Braeburn or any other slightly tart variety.

Leek and Potato Soup

Serves 4
3 leeks
A knob of butter
1 onion, chopped
4 large potatoes, peeled and chopped
20 oz/590 ml vegetable stock; add extra if needed
Salt and freshly ground black pepper
10 oz/295 ml heavy cream
Chopped fresh parsley

Chop the leeks and wash very carefully in several changes of salted water. Melt the butter in a large saucepan. Add the onion and fry gently for about 10 minutes, until cooked but still translucent. Add the leeks. Cook for another 5 minutes, then add the potatoes and vegetable stock and extra if necessary to cover. Season with salt and pepper to taste and cook for about 20 minutes, until the potatoes are done. Add the cream, garnish with parsley, and serve.

VARIATION

Vichyssoise. On a warm summer's day I like to make the leek and potato soup as above but I serve it really well chilled. The French call this vichyssoise. For a different garnish use chopped scallions.

Lentil Soup

This is a substantial lunch soup and goes very well with my Guinness Bread (page 91), which I'm sure you'll all enjoy.

Serves 6
1 Tbsp sunflower or canola oil
2 large potatoes, peeled and chopped
2 onions, chopped
3 carrots, peeled and chopped
1 celery stalk, chopped
40 oz/1.2 L vegetable stock
20 oz/590 ml water
12 oz/340 g red lentils, washed
1 small can tomato puree (10¾ oz/305 g)
2 garlic cloves, crushed
Salt and freshly ground black pepper
Heavy cream
Chopped fresh parsley

Heat the oil in a large saucepan and add the potato, onion, carrots, and celery. Cover with parchment paper and the pan lid and sweat gently over a low heat for about 10 minutes, until the onions are soft but not brown. Remove the parchment paper and add the stock, water, lentils, tomato puree, garlic, and salt and pepper to taste. Bring to the boil, reduce the heat to a slow simmer, and cook for about an hour, stirring occasionally. Liquidise the soup using a blender or food processor and season with salt and pepper to taste. Serve with a little swirl of cream and some parsley.

Kinky's Note:
Instead of vegetable stock use stock made with a ham bone.

Mussel and Seafood Chowder

Here is another very substantial lunch soup, especially when served with my Irish Wheaten Bread (page 94) and butter.

Serves 4

1 lb/455 g mussels, scallops, and peeled shrimp

8 oz/235 ml dry white wine

1½ lb/680 g skinless and boneless white fish, such as cod, haddock, or snapper

15 oz/445 ml milk

1 tsp fresh thyme leaves

1 bay leaf

Salt and freshly ground black pepper

1 Tbsp olive oil or sunflower oil

1 oz/28 g butter

4 oz/113 g bacon, chopped

1½ lb/680 g potatoes, peeled and finely diced

1 leek, washed and thinly sliced

1 small carrot, peeled and thinly sliced

1 shallot, minced

4 oz/120 ml heavy cream

1 Tbsp fish sauce (optional)

A handful of chopped fresh parsley

First, clean the mussels and, using a sharp knife, remove the beard. (That's the little tufty bit on the shell.) Bring the wine to the boil in a large saucepan, add the mussels, cover, and cook for about 4 minutes. Discard any that did not open and remove most of the rest from their shells, leaving just a few in the shell for decoration. Reserve the cooking liquid.

In another pan, simmer the fish in the milk with the thyme and bay leaf for just a few minutes until cooked but still firm. Remove the fish and set to one side. Discard the bay leaf and season the cooking liquid well with salt and pepper.

Now heat the oil and butter in a deep pan, add the bacon, and sauté until crisp. Add the potatoes, leek, carrot, and shallot. Cover and cook gently, without browning, for a few minutes. Add the cooking liquid from the mussels and the fish and simmer all together until the potatoes are soft and breaking up. (You may wish to blend this briefly with an immersion blender or process some of it in a blender or food processor if you think it looks too chunky.) Then add the scallops and shrimp. They will only need a very little time to cook so watch that you do not overcook them or they will become rubbery.

Finally, add the fish and the cooked mussels together with the cream and fish sauce. Season with salt and pepper to taste and add parsley. If the chowder is too thick just add some more milk or water and adjust the seasoning if necessary before serving.

Pea and Mint Soup

Serves 4

1 oz/28 g butter

1 small bunch scallions, chopped

1½ lb/680 g fresh peas, shelled, or frozen peas

25 oz/740 ml chicken stock or vegetable stock

A large handful of mint leaves, chopped, plus mint leaves for serving

Salt and freshly ground black pepper

8 oz/235 ml heavy cream or crème fraîche

Melt the butter in a large cooking pot and add the scallions. Sauté gently for a few minutes until soft. Then add the peas, stock, mint, and salt and pepper to taste. Boil for 3 or 4 minutes until the peas are cooked. Remove from the heat and allow to cool. Liquidise using a blender or food processor and chill. Mix in the cream and decorate with mint leaves before serving.

Kinky's Note:

This soup has a coarse texture but if you would prefer it to be smooth you could blend it for longer or push it through a sieve. And of course on days when the wind is howling like a stepmother's breath you can serve it hot.

Potato Soup

Serves 4

6 slices bacon, chopped, or 4 oz/113 g, chopped

2 oz/56 g butter

1 large onion, chopped

1 lb 2 oz/500 g russet potatoes, peeled and cut into cubes

25 oz/740 ml chicken stock or ham stock

1 bay leaf

Salt and freshly ground black pepper

4 Tbsp sour cream

4 Tbsp chopped fresh chives

Fry the bacon in the butter in a large heavy-bottomed pan until crisp. Remove from the pan and set to one side. In the buttery residue, fry the onion over a gentle heat until it is starting to go soft but not browned. Add the potatoes, cover with parchment paper and the pan lid, and sweat over a very low heat for 8 to 10 minutes, checking often to make sure that the vegetables are not sticking.

Discard the parchment. Add the stock, bay leaf, and salt and pepper to taste to the pan and bring to the boil. If any surface scum forms, just remove it with a slotted spoon. Reserve some bacon for a garnish and return the rest of the bacon to the pan and simmer, covered, for 20 minutes until the potatoes are cooked.

Remove the bay leaf and half the bacon and process using an immersion blender. (You can leave this as chunky as you like or make it smooth and creamy. If it is too thick just add a little milk.) Add salt if necessary. Garnish with the sour cream, chives, and reserved bacon, and serve.

Tomato Soup

Serves 4 to 6

1 Tbsp olive oil

2 onions, chopped

2 carrots, peeled and chopped

2 potatoes, peeled and chopped

2 lb/910 g ripe tomatoes, skinned and chopped, or equivalent weight in canned
tomatoes

34 oz/1 L vegetable stock or chicken stock (good-quality stock cubes are grand
for this)

1 garlic clove, crushed

1 tsp sugar

Salt and freshly ground black pepper

Chopped fresh basil or parsley

Heavy cream

Heat the oil in a large heavy-bottomed saucepan and add the onions, carrot, and potatoes. Cover and cook gently for about 10 minutes, until softened. Add the tomatoes
and cook for a further 5 minutes. Add the stock, garlic, and sugar and simmer for about
15 minutes. With an immersion blender or in a food processor, puree until smooth,
season with salt and pepper to taste, and serve with a swirl of cream and chopped basil.

Kinky's Note:

If using fresh tomatoes, immerse them in boiling water for a
minute then plunge them into ice cold water and draw a line
round the tomato with a sharp knife. This will make it easy to
peel off the skin. When I am in a hurry, I like to use the
canned tomatoes instead, which I think have a better flavor
anyway.

*D*octor Laverty told you in the introduction that I had asked him to write down some of his memories of 1964, the first year he worked with Doctor Fingal Flahertie O'Reilly. Barry told me that for a young man fresh from the sheltered world of boys' boarding school and the cloistered medical school, meeting our boss for the first time and moving into Number One Main Street, Ballybucklebo, in County Down could only be described as culture shock. The rural peaceful village itself and the surrounding country were certainly a refreshing change from Belfast city life. The region was populated with characters as diverse as Donall Donnelly, an arch trickster; Councillor Bertie Bishop, builder, Grand Master of the local Orange Lodge, and all-round bastard; Cissie Sloan, a woman with a heart of corn, but who never stopped talking; and Maggie MacCorkle, Barry's first patient, who complained of headaches—two inches above the crown of her head. Barry laughed at my request, but he did as I'd asked.

I did a bit of rewriting and here is the first story.

A
Source
of Innocent
Merriment

Doctor O'Reilly was an impatient man, but on occasions when faced with what he thought was someone showing off or being a smart Alec needing to be taught a lesson, he could bide until the time was absolutely right to give the subject their comeuppance. Then he'd pounce on the unsuspecting victim like one of those jumping spiders. I know because he did it to me.

In September of 1964, we had driven up to Belfast to attend a lecture at the Royal Victoria Hospital.

I'd only been working for him for a few weeks. Someone, and for once I can't quote my source, something which we had been trained to do as young doctors, but someone said, "A first impression is the one thing you don't get a second chance to make."

It had been that way when I had first met my illustrious senior. I'd been standing on his doorstep, having just rung the doorbell hoping to meet a rural GP who had advertised for an assistant. To my amazement the door had burst open. An ogre stood there and hurled a small man and a sock and shoe into a rose bush. "Next time, Seamus Galvin, you want me to look at a sore ankle, wash your bloody feet." You can imagine what my first impression of Doctor Fingal Flahertie O'Reilly, physician and surgeon, was and based on that I was determined to do my very best not to antagonise him. I also set out to show him that although I might be freshly minted, I really did know my stuff. Perhaps I tried too hard.

Now, to return to the lecture in question. Part of a series put on for GPs by the consultants at the teaching hospital, it concerned diseases like multiple sclerosis, cerebellar ataxia, and Friedrich's ataxia, all arcane neurological disorders. Ataxia, I should explain, is the inability to coordinate voluntary muscle movements.

The speaker said, "One diagnostic sign is the presence of dysdiadochokinesia . . ."

"Begob," whispered O'Reilly, who was giving the outward appearance of being bored silly, "if you put an air to that you could sing it."

I shushed him and tried to concentrate.

When the lecture finished and it was time for questions, I stuck up my hand and asked what I thought was an erudite one and, hoping to impress O'Reilly, cited Houston, Joiner, and Trounce; 1962, as the source of the information upon which the question and my subsequent elaboration were based. I stole a glance to see my senior frown, shake his head, and grunt. Perhaps I hadn't quite succeeded in having the effect I had intended.

Never mind. I was easily distracted when he said, "All the listening would give a fellah a thirst. Let's nip across the road to O'Kane's Pub before we drive home. I'd go a pint and a nibble."

"Fair enough," I said, falling into step for the short walk to the Grosvenor Road.

"Go on in," he said, holding open the door. The place was a fug of tobacco smoke, beery smells, and snatches of conversation. I knew the pub well because in my day it had been a favourite haunt of medical students and junior doctors.

In no time O'Reilly had ordered two pints of Guinness and asked to see the menu. "Fancy a bite?" he asked.

"No thanks." I shook my head. O'Reilly's appetite was famous, but I am a small man. Not three hours ago we'd polished off a dinner of Kinky's avocado mousse with shrimp, steak and kidney pie, and a cheese plate.

"Right," he said as the barman delivered our drinks. "Do you still do mussels in Guinness?"

"We do, sir."

"Grand. I'll have a plate."

As we waited for his grub I thought I'd have one more try to impress him. "I think," I said, "it really does add weight to your argument when you can cite your source." It didn't seem to have registered.

I forgot about the whole thing. I didn't find out until several weeks later that my comments had not gone unnoticed.

We were making a home visit to see a retired British army colonel who, stereotypical as it may seem, was suffering from gout.

Colonel James Fothergill-Smythe (Retired) was an aged artefact of the Anglo-Irish Ascendancy and had what the Scots would call a very good conceit of himself. Perhaps his pre-war years of service in India had led him to believe that he was king of the castle and that all others, his physicians included, were of the serving classes to be treated as a Russian dowager duchess might have treated one of her serfs. Florid of face, clipped grey moustache above a nose with as many broken veins as a sea anemone has tentacles, heavy of build, he barely deigned to greet us when we had been shown into his study by a maid who flinched every time the cantankerous old man spoke. "You, O'Reilly . . ." He didn't bother to acknowledge my presence, "are ten minutes late."

"Och," said O'Reilly, who was no respecter of rank or title, "sure in't it better late than never?"

The Colonel sat in a wingback chair, his heavily bandaged left foot propped up on a footstool. Beside his chair, a mahogany tabletop was supported on the amputated and preserved foot of an elephant. On the wood-panelled walls hung trophies of his Indian days—a scowling Bengal tiger's head, some unfortunate member of the deer family with twisted horns. There was a double-barrelled gun on supports. The thing had such a bore that I thought it probably fired two-pounder shells.

At O'Reilly's remark the colonel gave such a snort I wondered if, like Mowgli who was raised by wolves, the old man had had an Indian elephant for an *ayah*.

"Indeed," said O'Reilly, "and how's the hoof?"

"Blasted thing hurts like blazes. You quacks don't know your stuff."

"Mmm," said O'Reilly. "Better take a look." He squatted to do so.

"Get out, Margaret," the colonel ordered his maid who, not having been dismissed earlier, had stayed, presumably ready to dance at her master's slightest whim.

She fled.

I waited until O'Reilly had completed his examination of a red, swollen, glazed-looking big toe, reapplied swabs freshly soaked in *lotio plumbi et opii* (lead and opiate lotion), and gently redressed the toe and foot, all the while to the accompaniment of muttered imprecations from the colonel.

That O'Reilly did not respond surprised me. His initial instructions to me when I had accepted the job as his assistant had included his first law, "Never, never, never let the patient get the upper hand." Little did I know that the old colonel's foul temper was being tolerated because it was going to give O'Reilly the opportunity to take me down a peg or two after my being "Doctor Know-It-All" at the neurological lecture. Before pouncing on its prey, the jumping spider lines up its route of attack. So did O'Reilly.

He stood, walked to a desk, and scribbled on a prescription pad before returning and handing it to the colonel. "The colchicine's not doing its job. That's for prednisolone 10 milligrams. I want you to take three tablets at once and then one tablet every eight hours. I'll be back to see you in four days."

Before O'Reilly could take his leave, the old man was yelling, "Margaret, get in here you lazy girl. I want you to run to the chemist and get this prescription filled."

We left.

On the drive home, I ventured an opinion. "Perhaps it's the gout making him so cantankerous? Constant pain can do that."

"It hasn't made him any worse than he's always been," O'Reilly said. "Yells at his maid, browbeats his wife, is rude to shopkeepers. I don't let him get away with much, but I wanted you to see him for what he really is. He's nothing but a right old dastard."

I should have kept my mouth shut, but I said, "Don't you mean bastard?"

That "look out" gleam appeared in O'Reilly's dark eyes. "No," he said, narrowly missing a cyclist. "I mean exactly what I said. Dastard. Those poor unfortunates born out of wedlock and called bastards bear no responsibilty for their state. Bastards can't help it. Dastards have to work at it to get to be such miserable gobshites."

I laughed. "Well said. Nice turn of phrase."

"Ah, but I didn't coin it. It's not original. You remember that neurology lecture?"

"Yes." I frowned. I couldn't see where this was leading.

"And you waxing lyrical and telling me in the car afterward always to cite my sources? I got a feeling you were trying to impress me."

I began to feel a certain discomfort.

"Well, when it comes to bastards and dastards my source for that remark is the late, great, recently deceased Dubliner Brendan Behan; 1956. Impressed that I can cite my source?"

I confess my blush was as hot and the same shade as the colonel's left big toe.

"Och," said O'Reilly, "you're only young, Barry. We all did it when we were young. You'll learn. No offence was taken . . ."

But a lesson had been learned by me.

"And I tell you what," said O'Reilly. "As that's the last visit of the day I'll show you I mean it. We'll go to the Mucky Duck, and I'll let you buy me a pint."

He'd let me pay for it. All I could think of, tongue-in-cheek of course, was, Doctor Fingal Flahertie O'Reilly, when you want to make a point sometimes you can be a right dastard, too.

Light Plates

I'm after calling these "light plates" although some of them are not. Some might also be served before a meal and you could then call them "starters." However, if you just have them on their own they will also make adequate lunch dishes. Picnics are always popular in Ireland in spite of the weather, and as most of these are easily wrapped in Irish linen tea towels and packed into wicker baskets, they make great picnic fare. Doctor O' Reilly just loved to take Scotch eggs with him when he went shooting. It was, he said, like taking a picnic breakfast of egg and sausage. I always preferred to have them hot but you can make up your own mind.

Chicken Liver Pâté

Serves 4 to 6

12 oz/340 g chicken livers

1 Tbsp sunflower oil

140 gm / 5 oz softened butter

2 shallots, finely chopped

1 garlic clove, crushed

½ tsp finely chopped fresh thyme or ¼ tsp dried thyme

2 Tbsp brandy

2 Tbsp port

Salt and freshly ground black pepper

Fresh parsley sprigs

Wash and pat dry the livers on paper towels. Remove any little blood vessels. Heat the oil and a knob of butter in a heavy-bottomed frying pan over a gentle heat. Add the livers gradually so that they brown but do not toughen. Cook for about 5 minutes, turning once. They should still be pink in the centre. Remove from the pan and set aside. Now put the pan back over a low heat and sauté the shallots, garlic, and thyme for a minute or so in the residue. Finally add the brandy and port and deglaze the pan with the liquid.

Now put everything into a food processor, add salt and pepper and the remainder of the softened butter, and process until smooth. Chill in individual ramekin dishes, decorate each with a sprig of parsley, and serve with wheaten or fresh white crusty bread or crackers.

Scotch Eggs

These keep well in the fridge for a couple of days. And sure doesn't himself like to take these in the game bag when he goes on a shoot?

Serves 4
5 eggs
8 oz/227 g sausage meat
1 scallion, chopped
1 Tbsp chopped fresh parsley
1 tsp chopped fresh thyme
Salt and freshly ground black pepper
4 oz/113 g dried or panko bread crumbs
1 Tbsp seasoned flour
Vegetable or canola oil for frying

Hard-boil four eggs for about 10 minutes and cool them quickly in cold running water. Then peel off the shells. Mix the sausage meat with the scallion, parsley, thyme, a little salt, and plenty of pepper and make into four flattened ovals on a floured work surface. Beat the remaining egg in a shallow dish. Put the bread crumbs in another shallow dish. Coat the cooked eggs with the seasoned flour and wrap the sausage meat around each egg, making sure to seal each egg completely. Coat with the beaten egg and then with the crumbs.

Now heat the oil in a deep frying pan or wok to 350°F/180°C to 375°F/190°C. (If you do not have a thermometer you can test the temperature by dropping a small cube of bread into the oil and if it sizzles and turns golden brown then the oil is hot enough. Please be very careful with the hot oil and never turn your back on it.) Carefully lower the eggs, two at a time, into the hot oil and cook for 8 to 10 minutes, until the sausage meat is a nice brown colour and thoroughly cooked. Repeat with the remaining egg.

Remove with a slotted spoon and drain on kitchen paper. Allow to cool and serve with a salad.

Kinky's Note:

Cooling hard-boiled eggs quickly under cold running water will prevent them from discoloring.

Veal Liver Pâté

Serves 4 to 6

10 oz/284 g calf's liver

Enough milk to cover the liver

1 Tbsp sunflower oil

4 oz/113 g butter, softened

2 shallots, finely chopped

1 garlic clove, crushed

½ tsp finely chopped fresh thyme or ¼ tsp dried thyme

2 Tbsp brandy

1 Tbsp lemon juice

Salt and freshly ground black pepper

Chopped fresh parsley

Soak the liver in the milk for several hours or overnight. Pat dry on paper towels. Remove any little blood vessels. In a frying pan, heat the oil and a knob of the butter over a gentle heat and add the livers gradually so that they brown. Cook for about 5 minutes, turning once. Remove from the pan and set aside. Put the pan back on the heat and cook the shallots, garlic, and thyme for a minute or two in the buttery residue. Finally, add the brandy and lemon juice and deglaze the pan with the liquid.

Now put the rest of the butter, the liver, and the contents of the pan into a food processor, season with salt and pepper, and process until smooth. Divide into individual ramekin dishes and chill. Serve garnished with parsley, with Wheaten Bread (page 94) or fresh Potato and Pumpkin Seed Bread (page 96).

Fishy Starters

Sea fishing around the coast of Ireland has always been abundant and of great importance to the Irish and I do think there are probably as many legends and myths about fish as there are rivers and lakes in Ireland.

One such story I learned at my mother's knee was about Fintan, the salmon of knowledge. It was said that the first taste of this fish would impart all the knowledge in the world to the recipient. The Irish poet Fineigas had spent seven years up and down the Boyne River trying to catch the salmon. When at last he finally succeeded, he gave the fish to his pupil, the young Finn MacCool, to cook, warning him that he was not to taste it. As Finn was cooking the fish, a blister appeared on its skin and Finn pressed down on this with his thumb. Instinctively he sucked his thumb to relieve the pain, thus becoming the first to taste the salmon and receive the gift of knowledge.

Avocado Mousse with Shrimp

Serves 4

3 avocadoes, peeled and pitted

8 oz/227 g cream cheese

6 oz/170 g finely chopped celery

4 oz/120 ml heavy cream

2 Tbsp chopped scallion

Juice of 1 lime

3 drops Tabasco

1 envelope gelatin

4 oz/120 ml cold water

Salt and freshly ground black pepper

8 oz/227 g cooked, peeled shrimp or prawns

Blend the avocadoes, cream cheese, celery, cream, and scallion together in a large bowl. Mix in the lime juice and Tabasco. Dissolve the gelatin in the water and stir into the avocado mixture. Season with salt and pepper to taste and fold in three quarters of the shrimp. Now you can either put it into a large mould (about 1 L) or individual ramekin dishes and chill until needed. Unmould and serve sliced on a bed of lamb's lettuce and watercress garnished with the remaining shrimp.

Gravadlax, Irish-Style

This has to be easier than just about anything else in this cookbook and takes no time at all. (Use Atlantic salmon if you can get it, for isn't that the fish we eat in Ireland? And didn't I tell you that Finn MacCool ate Fintan the salmon of knowledge and gained all the wisdom in the world?)

Serves 8

1 (1-lb/455-g) centre-cut skin-on salmon fillet, pinbones removed

Juice of 2 limes or lemons, plus lemon wedges for serving

1 Tbsp sea salt

1 Tbsp sugar

1 large bunch fresh dill

Cucumber slices for decoration

1 Tbsp capers

Cut the salmon into two pieces and lay one piece skin-side down in a deep dish or a loaf tin, lined with cling film. Mix the lime juice, salt, and sugar together. Reserve some of the dill for a garnish and finely chop the rest of the dill. Spread half of the chopped dill over the fish in the dish. Place the rest of the fish on top, skin-side up, and cover with the remaining dill. Pour the juice mixture over the salmon. Bring the sides of the cling film over the top to seal it. Now place a weight on top of the cling wrap. (Just whatever you have handy, such as a couple of tins of baked beans or anything else that feels just as heavy, would do.) Place in the fridge and leave for a total time of 24 to 36 hours. The fish "cooks" or "cures" in the sweet, acidic juice. I think it helps if you remove the weights and turn it over once, then replace the weights and leave to finish curing.

Remove from the fridge and rinse both pieces of salmon in ice-cold water to wash off most of the dill. Then pat it dry between sheets of paper towels. Place the fish on a cutting board and slice into very thin slices, removing it from the skin as you cut. A very sharp knife is required. Arrange on a plate and decorate with the cucumber slices, capers, reserved dill fronds, and lemon wedges. Serve with buttered Irish Wheaten Bread (page 94) and freshly ground pepper to accompany.

VARIATION

Serves 4

Gravadlax Bon-Bon. If you have a smaller piece of salmon or a trout fillet then this is an alternative. Remove the skin and make a mix, as before, of lemon or lime juice, sugar, and salt and some very finely chopped dill. Lay the fish in this for an hour or so. Then place the fish on a piece of cling film and roll up tightly, twisting and sealing the edges, like you would for a bon-bon. Leave for a few hours or overnight, then remove the cling film and slice thinly so it looks like a Swiss roll. Serve with Horseradish Cream or Mustard Sauce (recipes follow). Decorate with salad leaves, lemon wedges, and bread or crackers.

Horseradish Cream

Serves 8

4 oz/113 g crème fraîche
1 Tbsp prepared horseradish
1 tsp Dijon mustard

Mix all the ingredients together.

Mustard Sauce

    4 oz/113 g crème fraîche

    2 tsp Dijon mustard or more, to taste

Mix the crème fraîche and mustard together.

GUINNESS

I do think only the shamrock is more Irish than good old Liffey Water, as Guinness used to be known. And sure no surprise there. Wasn't it first brewed by Mister Arthur Guinness at Saint James's Gate on the banks of the Liffey? He made three dark beers: single stout (a word which was a measure of the ale's strength), double stout, and export stout. The single stout was also known as "plain." Flan O'Brian immortalised it in his poem *The Workman's Friend* in the line "A pint of plain is your only man." Himself told me that after about ninety years, the brewery was selling 350,000 barrels a year, and by 1886 that had risen to nearly a million and a half.

And it has more uses than as just a drink. Women who had had babies were given a bottle a day to help them make milk and patients in hospitals got a third of a pint a day as a tonic. It was donated by the brewery, and young doctors would sweetheart senior nurses into ordering extra when the scallywags wanted to have a party.

And cooks like me found all kinds of uses for it. The recipe below is one but there are others in this book, so. I hope you enjoy them all.

Mussels in Guinness

Serves 4 to 6

2¼ lb/1 kg mussels

A knob of butter

2 shallots, diced

10 oz/295 ml Guinness

8 oz/235 ml fish stock

1 bay leaf

A good splash of heavy cream

1 Tbsp chopped fresh dill or parsley

Lemon wedges

First, clean the mussels and, using a sharp knife, remove the beards. (That's the little tufty bit on the shell.) Melt the butter in a large saucepan over medium heat, add the shallots, and sauté until just soft. Add the Guinness, stock, and bay leaf and simmer until reduced by half. Add the cream and reduce a little more before adding the mussels. Cover and cook for 2 or 3 minutes, by which time the shells should have opened. Discard any that have not. Sprinkle with the dill and serve in bowls with lemon wedges and Irish Wheaten Bread (page 94).

Kinky's Note:

I like to serve this with a soup spoon on the side, as the cooking liquid is a delicious broth and it would be a shame to waste it, so.

VARIATION

You can of course make this in the more traditional French way by substituting a dry white wine for the Guinness, adding a clove of garlic and a tied bunch of thyme.

Remove the thyme before serving with crusty French bread. The French like to use the liquor as a soup and the bread to mop up any remaining juices.

Smoked Mackerel Pâté

Serves 4 to 6

1 lb/4 to 5 fresh mackerel

7 oz/200 g cream cheese

Juice of 2 lemons, plus lemon wedges for serving

1 Tbsp chopped fresh parsley, plus extra for serving

1 tsp chopped fresh thyme

Freshly ground black pepper

I like to barbeque the mackerel for this recipe because mackerel is a very oily fish and cooking it this way releases the oil and also gives the fish a nice smoky flavour. Keep the skin on the fish and remove when cold.

Remove the bones and place the mackerel in a blender with the cream cheese, lemon juice, parsley, thyme, and pepper to taste. Blend until roughly mixed or make it smooth if you prefer. Put into individual 6-ounce/180 ml ramekins and garnish with parsley. Serve with lemon wedges and toast.

Smoked Salmon with Cream Cheese

Whilst you can use your own "cured" gravadlax for this, I think it holds together better using store-bought smoked salmon and, as the cure is more strongly flavoured, it is tempered by the mild taste of the cream cheese.

Serves 4 to 6

2 Tbsp finely chopped fresh dill

12 oz/340 g sliced smoked salmon

4 oz/113 g cream cheese, softened

2 oz/56 g crème fraîche

2 oz/56 g scallions, chopped

Juice of 1 lemon, plus lemon wedges for serving

1 Tbsp capers

Freshly ground black pepper

Cover a rectangular plate with cling film, allowing a generous amount to extend over the edges. Spread most of the dill on the cling film and lay the smoked salmon on top so that there are no spaces between the slices.

Combine the cream cheese, crème fraîche, scallions, lemon juice, and remaining dill in a small bowl. Spread this mixture on the smoked salmon. Using the cling film to lift the salmon, bring up one side so that the cheese is now covered completely by the salmon, rather like a sandwich. Twist the two ends of the cling film so that the shape looks like a giant sausage or a Christmas cracker. Now chill overnight in the fridge.

When you want to serve it, carefully remove the plastic and, using a sharp knife, cut it into ½-inch/12-mm slices. Place on an oblong serving dish with lemon wedges and capers and season with pepper. Serve with buttered Irish Wheaten Bread (page 94) or crisp crackers.

Smoked Salmon Pâté

Serves 4

6 oz/170 g smoked salmon

2½ oz/70 g cream cheese, softened

2½ oz/70 g crème fraîche

2 oz/56 g fresh bread crumbs

1 Tbsp horseradish or slightly less wasabi

1 Tbsp chopped fresh dill

To garnish: 1 Tbsp capers and lemon wedges

Combine all the ingredients except the capers and lemon wedges in a blender and blend until smooth. Spoon into individual ramekins, cover with cling film, and refrigerate. Serve with lemon wedges and capers, accompanied by crackers, toast, or Irish Wheaten Bread (page 94).

Strangford Sea Scallops
Marinated with Mango, Avocado, and Chili Salsa

This beautiful dish was given to me by Paul McKnight, the executive chef of the Culloden Hotel. Culloden Estate and Spa, 1 Bangor Road, Holywood. Co. Down. N Ireland.

Serves 6 to 8
Juice of 2 limes
1 Tbsp good-quality olive oil
A pinch of superfine sugar
1 ripe avocado, peeled, pitted, and finely diced
1 ripe mango, peeled and pitted
½ red bell pepper
2 scallions, finely shredded
One small red chili, seeded and finely chopped
8 large scallops, coral (tendon) removed (must be fresh)
Flaky sea salt, such as Maldon, and freshly ground black pepper
Chopped fresh cilantro

Cut each scallop horizontally into 4 thin slices, arrange on plate overlapping to form a circle.

Cut avocado, mango, and pepper into small neat dice. Mix with juice of two limes, olive oil, superfine sugar, scallions, and red chili to make dressing.

Season the scallops with salt and pepper.

Spoon the dressing over the scallops, leave to marinate for 5 to 10 minutes.

Before serving, sprinkle with chopped cilantro or with micro cilantro.

Tuna Tartare

Serves 4

8 oz/227 g raw tuna steak, chopped

Grated zest and juice of 1 lime or lemon

2 avocadoes, peeled, pitted, and chopped

3 oz/85 g cucumber, peeled and chopped

1 oz/28 g red or white salad onion, chopped

½ tsp wasabi or horseradish

Chopped fresh cilantro or dill

Marinate the tuna overnight in the refrigerator in the lime juice and zest.

Add the avocadoes, cucumber, onion, and wasabi and mix everything together. Plate using a ring to make a little tower. (Alternatively, use a silicone mold.) Sprinkle each tower with cilantro and finish each plate with mixed lettuce leaves lightly dressed with lime juice and olive oil.

Kinky's Note:

When serving fish raw, always use fish that has been frozen, as this destroys any parasites that may have been present.

The Grave's
a Fine and
Private Place

We had just finished one of Kinky's "shmall little" dinners—creamy lentil soup, steak and mushroom pie with Brussels sprouts and carrots. Dessert had been Eton Mess topped with whipped cream. Totally replete, I would have been happy to sit for a while gently digesting, but one of O'Reilly's patients needed him and so off we'd set.

Outside the big speeding Rover car, it was one of those gentle early summer evenings in Ulster. Cotton wool clouds too lazy to scud drifted across a sky of robin's eggshell blue, and the sun—not yet the fiery orb of mid-July and August—warmed the salt-and-clover-perfumed air and stitched flashing sequins on the ripples of Belfast Lough. Out on the water, a small fleet of Fairy yachts, sailing dinghys with secret aspirations to grow into bigger boats, tacked and jostled for position before the start of one of the Royal North of Ireland Yacht Club's evening races off the village of Cultra.

Inside the car was different, and akin to the inside of a steel foundry: hot, smoky, and tense, as Doctor Fingal Flahertie O'Reilly's briar belched Erinmore Flake tobacco fumes. I wound down the window and clung on to the sides of my seat as he hurled the juggernaut into a hairpin bend. I muttered, "Slow down," under my breath and had about as much influence on his driving as a wren would if it tried to tackle a bull head-on.

"I'm worried," O'Reilly said.

Not nearly as much as I was, but my concern was merely for my life. His was about an entirely different matter. "Maggie Mac-Corkle just told me something about Neill McLoughlin and I want to make sure he's all right. The poor man must be worried stiff."

And when O'Reilly was worried about one of his patients, a squadron of Centurion main battle tanks would not have stood in his way.

I hunched down in my seat and recalled the details of matters leading up to his current concern. The story is convoluted, but bear with me and I'll try to explain. It revolves around both the superstitious nature of the Irish and the basic pragmatism of the Ulsterman.

Nearly a year ago, I had been introduced to a couple who had been married for forty-odd years. And odd they must have been. Neill McLoughlin, who farmed up in the Ballybucklebo Hills, was a small man, balding, soft-spoken, self-effacing. His wife, Cecily, was brawny and florid-faced, and might have been described by the English as either a virago or a termagant. In Ulster she qualified as being a "right ould targe" who dominated her husband. Just as O'Reilly was instantly obeyed by his Labrador, Arthur Guinness, Cecily could make Neill come to heel by fixing him with a sub-Arctic stare and saying one word, "Neill," in a voice as loaded with venom as the sacs of a king cobra. How he'd stuck it for so long was a mystery to everyone in the village of Ballybucklebo.

O'Reilly braked, stopped, and said, "Get out. We'll walk. It's quicker. And I'll explain as we go."

I followed. There was a back lane to the farmhouse.

"The drive for cars and farm vehicles is at the other side of the farm and we'd need to drive about four miles to get to it," he said.

"Fine by me," I said, falling into step. The grass crushed by our footsteps gave off a new-mown hay scent, and I could make out the fluted phrases, repeated six times, of a mistle thrush high in a leafy sycamore growing at the end of the lane.

"You know that Cecily died eight months ago?" O'Reilly asked.

"I did," I said. "In the Royal Victoria Hospital. Cerebral aneurysm, as I recall. Unexpected and sudden." When a weakness of one of the arteries inside the brain burst, death could be rapid. "She regained consciousnes for a day but . . ." I shrugged. "I seem to remember Neill was pretty stoical about it."

"De mortuis nihil nisi bonum . . ." O'Reilly said.

"Speak nothing but good of the dead, from the original Greek translated into Latin in the fifteenth century. We had to learn it at school."

"Quite," O'Reilly said, "but the tag doesn't stop me observing that the dearness of the departed may have left something to be desired and that Neill wasn't so much exhibiting a stiff upper lip as evincing a great deal of relief. A least that was what was widely believed in the village, and there was great deal of empathy for the man." O'Reilly plucked a long grass stem to stick between his teeth. "We can be a pretty understanding lot, Ulsterfolk, and it was a combination of that and our archaic superstitiousness that brought Maggie MacCorkle round to see me a wee while back."

"Go on," I said.

"It seems, and it's common knowledge, that in the last month Neill has started walking out with the widow Carmichael." O'Reilly removed the grass stem. "Maggie told me that there's a belief that Neill is going to propose to the widow."

"More power to his wheel," I said, pleased for them. "And I'll bet that everybody approves." I frowned. "I don't see what Maggie would be concerned about."

"That," said O'Reilly, "is where the superstition comes in. Apparently Cissie Sloan told Aggie Arbuthnot, Aggie told Flo Bishop, and she told Maggie that a patient in the next bed heard Cecily yell at Neill the afternoon before she died that if she went to join the choir invisible and he married again she'd dig herself up from her grave and come to haunt him."

That stopped me in my tracks. Coincidentally, the song of the mistle thrush stopped, too. Silence.

O'Reilly said, "Even dead, she'll be making the man's life miserable. He'll believe he's accursed. He'd have saved himself a lot of trouble if he'd had her cremated, but you know how country folks feel about that. Our job, at least mine, is to try and get him to see sense. Stop worrying. And it'll take tact and delicacy."

Which, as I had seen repeatedly, were hardly Doctor Fingal Flahertie O'Reilly's long suits.

"Come on," he said and strode off.

I nodded and started to walk the last few yards to the back door of the McLoughlin farmhouse. We were greeted by a barking border collie. The dog's racket must have alerted Neill, who opened the back door, said quietly, "Wheest now, Jock. Into your kennel," waited until the dog had obeyed, and then said, "Come ahead doctors. Old Jock won't hurt you." He looked around and remarked, "Brave evening, for the time of year it's in."

We were shown into a spacious kitchen. Neither the range nor the turf fire were lit. The tidy tile-floored room smelled of furniture polish and fried lambs' liver, bacon, and onions that Neill would have cooked for his tea. "Please sit down," he said, indicating two arm chairs, and when we were seated asked, "Now what can I do for youse?"

This was definitely O'Reilly's problem, so I said nothing. Simply watched and listened.

"Um," said O'Reilly, whipping out his half-moon spectacles and perching them on his bent nose, "please understand, Mister McLoughlin, neither Doctor Laverty nor I wish to intrude."

Mister McLoughlin smiled and said, "Sure how could you do that, sir? Haven't yiz been my doctor since after the war? You likely know more about me than I do."

The man was certainly making it easy for O'Reilly to broach what for that time in Ulster would have been a delicate matter.

"It seems," O'Reilly said, "that when your wife was on her deathbed someone overheard her, ahem, put a curse on you."

The man's smile faded. "That's right, so it is," he said. "Mind you, no harm to her, but the way Cecily spoke, never mind hearing in the next bed. They likely heard her the whole length of the Grosvenor Road."

I hid a smile, but O'Reilly said, "Would you mind telling me what the curse was?"

"Mind? Not at all."

I frowned. In my experience, country Ulsterfolk took the supernatural very seriously. Neill McLoughlin didn't seem one bit put out.

"Please go ahead," O'Reilly said, leaning back and steepling his fingers.

"She tell me if I ever looked at another woman she'd dig her way up and come and haunt me."

"And," O'Reilly said, "I'm guessing it's got you pretty worried because . . ."

"Excuse me for interrupting, sir, because I'm walking out with Molly Carmichael?"

"Well, I, that is . . ." O'Reilly frowned.

I confess so did I. With most Ulstermen, O'Reilly would have been right on the money. They would have been terrified.

O'Reilly said, in his most professional manner, "I can reassure you that medically, scientifically coming back to haunt you, that would be quite impossible."

"That's very kind of you doctor, sir, to try til comfort me. Very kind indeed. And you're right, you know . . ."

I saw O'Reilly relax, smile.

"Because even if you're wrong . . ."

O'Reilly stiffened.

"Mister Coffin the undertaker'd heard the rumour too. He's got a heart of corn, that man. He seen I was dead worried, but told me there was a solution, so there was. And he made the funeral arrangements."

I remembered seeing the strangely named village undertaker before. The poor man had an enormous rhinophyma, a condition of blockage of the sebaceous glands of his nose that made him look like Chuckles the Clown wearing only one piece of stage makeup.

O'Reilly whipped off his half-moons and leant forward.

I waited to hear about counterspells with getting moss from the skull of a recently buried murderer, "eye of newt, toe of frog, wool of bat, tongue of dog," that kind of stuff, but the pragmatic answer that Mister Coffin had come up with was blinding in its simplicity.

O'Reilly said in a hushed voice, "And?"

"Mister Coffin said, and I was happy til agree, 'If that's the case we can fix that. We'll bury her facedown.'"

O'Reilly said, "What?" and started to chuckle.

"Aye," said Neill McLoughlin, "and if Cecily's heard I've proposed til Molly Carmichael, which I have and she's accepted, and Cecily's got started already," he paused, I think for effect, before saying, "she's got one hell of a long way to go."

Bread

Homemade bread in Ireland was traditionally soda bread made with soft wheat flour, buttermilk, and bicarbonate of soda (baking soda). Ma seemed to make it every day and I loved to watch. It took no time at all, just a few little minutes, and she never weighed the ingredients but sure didn't it always turn out just perfect.

The buttermilk was delivered to the door by "the Buttermilk Man" on his horse and cart. Ma would take an enamel jug out to have it filled from the large steel urn on the back of the cart. Sometimes the horse would leave behind a little gift, which Ma said was very good for the roses as she shovelled it up.

Of course the bread was delicious, while it was still hot from the baking, with the homemade jam that Ma made with raspberries and strawberries from the garden and blackberries picked in the autumn from the hedgerows in the country lanes by me and my sisters.

Barmbrack

This was a traditional sweet bread made at Halloween, and often a ring or silver charms would have been wrapped in greaseproof paper and placed in the mixture before baking. The lucky ingredients included a gold ring (usually a brass curtain ring) to foretell marriage; a silver threepenny bit or a sixpence to forecast wealth; a thimble to forecast spinsterhood; and a button to forecast bachelorhood. This is normally eaten toasted with butter and is much nicer if you can keep it for a day in an airtight tin.

Makes 1
12 oz/340 g mixed dried fruit
4½ oz/127 g soft brown sugar
9 oz/265 ml brewed black tea
3½ Tbsp whiskey
8 oz/227 g all-purpose flour
1 egg, beaten
2 tsp baking powder
½ tsp pumpkin pie spice (optional)
1 Tbsp/ 15 ml honey to glaze

Soak the fruit and sugar in the tea and whiskey overnight. The next day, preheat the oven to 325°F/170°C. Grease a 9 by 5-inch/23 by 12-cm loaf tin (or two smaller loaf tins). (In Ireland this was traditionally made in a round tin about 6 to 7 inches in diameter.) Mix in the flour and egg with the dried fruit, mixture of whiskey and tea, baking powder, and pumpkin pie spice (if you like it spicy) and mix well. Turn into the tin and bake for 1 hour (less if using smaller tins). Turn the loaf out onto a wire rack to cool, then melt the honey and brush the top of the loaf to give it a fine glaze.

Buttermilk Pancakes

Makes 10 to 14, depending on thickness

8 oz/227 g all-purpose flour

2 oz/56 g sugar

¼ tsp salt

2 eggs

1 tsp baking soda

10 oz/295 ml buttermilk

2 oz/56 g butter, melted, plus extra for the pan

Sift the flour, sugar, and salt into a large bowl. In a separate bowl, whisk the eggs. Dissolve the baking soda in the buttermilk. Now add the melted butter, beaten eggs, and buttermilk progressively to the flour mixture, beating until there are no lumps. If you leave this to sit in the refrigerator for 10 minutes the batter will be smoother. Just give it another stir. It should look quite thick; however, if you think it is too thick, just add a little more buttermilk.

Grease a large frying pan with a little butter for the first pancake only and heat over a medium heat. Pour enough batter into the hot pan to make a 6-inch/15-cm pancake. When the beady bubbles burst on the surface of the pancake it is time to flip it over and cook the other side. The second side will only take a minute or less and you may need to reduce the heat too. Leave the pancake on a wire rack to cool or keep warm to serve. Continue with the remaining batter. These pancakes freeze very well.

Soda Farls

The word "farl" comes from the Scots word *fardel,* meaning "fourth." The bread was shaped into a round and cut into four quarters and cooked on a griddle over an open fire. Nowadays I use a large frying pan instead. They take no time at all to make and are cooked in a shmall little minute.

Makes 4
8 oz/227 g all-purpose flour
½ tsp baking soda
½ tsp salt
1½ Tbsp butter
10 oz/295 ml buttermilk

First warm a griddle or a large frying pan over a medium heat and dust with a little flour. This will stop the wet dough mixture from sticking to the pan.

Sift the flour, baking soda, and salt into a bowl and rub in the butter. Now make a well in the middle and pour in about three-quarters of the buttermilk, stirring quickly. (The baking soda will react on contact with the buttermilk as the leavening agent, and if you take too long at this step the bread will not rise sufficiently.) Add the remaining buttermilk if needed. While the mixture should be quite wet and sticky it is not as wet as a pancake mixture would be. It should not be too wet and sloppy or you will not be able to shape it. Now if it still looks a little too wet to shape add some more flour gradually until it is like a bread dough and not a pancake batter. Now turn your dough out onto a well-floured work surface and knead lightly, then shape into a flat round.

Cut the dough into four wedges (farls) and place on the griddle. They should take 5 to 10 minutes on each side. Just to be sure they are cooked through to the centre, you could test with a skewer. Now put the farls on their edges and turn them every few minutes so that the side edges are cooked, too. This is called *harning.* Allow to cool on a wire rack under a slightly damp Irish linen teacloth. These can be frozen until required.

Kinky's Note:

1. These farls are very quick to make but if you are in a hurry you could substitute vegetable oil for butter and add with the buttermilk. If you cannot find buttermilk in the store you could use sweet milk with the addition of a teaspoonful of cream of tartar and a little lemon juice.

2. However you make it, no self-respecting Ulster Fry (page 111) should ever be without a soda farl. The farl is cut in half and fried in the bacon fat until it is crisp on both sides.

VARIATIONS

Treacle Farls: substitute molasses or treacle for 1 to 2 tablespoons of the buttermilk.
Wheaten Farls: use whole-wheat flour instead or a combination of whole-wheat and all-purpose flour.

Guinness Bread

Makes 2

1 Tbsp baking soda

8 oz/235 ml milk

10 oz/284 g all-purpose flour

10 oz/284 g whole-wheat flour

6 oz/170 g old-fashioned rolled oats

2 oz/56 g sunflower seeds

4 Tbsp brown sugar

1 Tbsp salt

15 oz/445 ml Guinness

2 Tbsp cooking oil

2 Tbsp molasses or treacle

Preheat the oven to 400°F/200°C. Grease two 9 by 5-inch (23 by 12-cm) loaf tins well, line them with parchment paper, and grease the parchment. Dissolve the baking soda in the milk. Mix the flours, oats, sunflower seeds, sugar, and salt in a large bowl, make a well in the centre, and add the Guinness followed by the oil and molasses. Lastly, add the milk gradually. (You add the milk last because sometimes you may need to add more or less depending on the brand of flour used or even the weather conditions. However, what you are aiming for is a nice soft dropping consistency.)

Divide the mixture between the loaf tins. (I ususally make 2 because the loaf freezes well and I always have one for an emergency.) Bake for 15 minutes, then turn the oven down to 350°F/180°C and bake for a further 35 to 45 minutes. The bread will sound hollow when the bottom is knocked. Turn the loaves out onto a wire rack to cool and cover with a damp tea towel.

Kinky's Note:

1. If you use the spoon to measure the oil first, the molasses will run off the spoon more easily.
2. Flour is a little bit like a sponge and it can absorb moisture from the atmosphere. Miss Sue Nolan, the school mistress, is very learnéd in these matters and she tells me that the amount of moisture in flour can vary because of damp weather and humidity in the atmosphere. How you store flour also makes a difference.

Irish Potato Bread

This is a great way of using up leftover mashed potatoes and takes no time at all to make. Also called potato farls, Irish Potato Bread is traditionally served with an Ulster Fry (page 111) and may be frozen until needed.

Makes 4
1 lb/455 g potatoes, cooked and mashed
4 oz/113 g all-purpose flour
1 oz/28 g butter, softened
½ tsp salt

While the potatoes are still warm, mash together with the other ingredients, then knead and roll on a floured board into a flat round. Cut into four farls (from the old Scots word *fardel,* meaning "fourth"), and place on a hot, lightly greased frying pan of a size large enough to accommodate them. Cook on both sides until golden brown. Allow to cool on a wire rack. Reheat in a dry pan or toaster, or in the microwave.

Irish Wheaten Bread

This is also known as Irish soda bread or brown bread.

Makes 2
10 oz/284 g all-purpose flour
10 oz/284 g whole-wheat flour
6 oz/170 g old-fashioned rolled oats
2 oz/56 g sunflower seeds or pumpkin seeds
2 Tbsp sugar
1 Tbsp salt
2 Tbsp butter or sunflower or canola oil, optional
1 Tbsp baking soda
1 tsp cream of tartar
34 oz/1 L buttermilk (or slightly less)

Preheat the oven to 400°F/200°C. Grease two 9 by 5-inch (23 by 12-cm) loaf tins well, line them with parchment paper, and grease the parchment. Mix the flours, oats, sunflower seeds, sugar, and salt in a large bowl. Rub the butter in with your fingertips. (If you are using oil, add it with the buttermilk.) Make a well in the centre of the dry ingredients. Dissolve the baking soda and cream of tartar in a cup of buttermilk. This will froth up so pour it into the flour mixture quickly (along with the oil, if using). You add the remaining milk gradually because sometimes you may need to add more or less depending on the brand of flour used or even the weather conditions. However, what you are aiming for is a nice soft dropping consistency.

Divide the mixture between the loaf tins. Make an indent down the centre of the dough with the blade of a knife. Bake for 15 minutes, then turn the oven down to 350°F/180°C and bake for a further 35 to 45 minutes. The bread will sound hollow when the bottom is knocked. Turn the bread out onto a wire rack to cool and cover with a damp tea towel.

You can make variations by adding or substituting various ingredients. I sometimes add more whole-wheat flour than all-purpose flour or different seeds. Adding molasses gives a rich brown color. I even add crushed garlic if I'm planning to use the bread as an accompaniment with soup or a savory starter. Ma never weighed her ingredients. Like a lot of Irish cooks she just used handfuls and instinctively knew when it was right.

Kinky's Note:

If you are using molasses, measure it with the same spoon that you used for the oil and it will slide off easily.

Potato and Pumpkin
Seed Bread

Makes 2

15 oz/445 ml warm water

1 Tbsp olive oil

1 Tbsp dried yeast

A pinch of sugar

1 lb 2 oz/500 g all-purpose flour

12 oz/340 g mashed potato

2 oz/56 g pumpkin seeds (or more if you like)

1½ tsp salt

Mix together the warm water, oil, yeast, and sugar in a jug and leave for about 10 minutes, until the mixture becomes frothy. Combine the flour, potato, and sunflower seeds in the bowl of a stand mixer. Using the dough hook, mix the liquid into the flour and potato.

Remove the bowl from the mixer, cover with a damp cloth or oiled cling film, and leave to rise in a warm place for about 2 hours or so. An airing cupboard is a good place. Or heat the oven to its lowest temperature and turn off. Providing that the residual low heat is not too warm, this should start the fermentation process without actually cooking the dough.

Preheat the oven to 450°F/230°C. Grease two 9 by 5-inch (23 by 12-cm) loaf tins well, line them with parchment paper, and grease the parchment. The dough will have risen now and you need to knock it back to take out the excess air. You can use the hook again or put it on a floured work surface and punch it about.

Transfer the dough to the tins and again leave covered with oiled cling film in a warm place until the dough has risen to the top of the tins, 15 to 30 minutes. Bake for about 35 minutes or until the top is golden brown. The bread will sound hollow when the bottom is knocked. Turn the loaves out onto a wire rack to cool and cover with a damp tea towel.

Kinky's Note:

If you are letting the dough rise in a warm oven or a bread-proofing oven programme, it really gives the rising process a head start if you create steam by placing a baking tin containing boiling water in the floor of the oven.

Potato-Apple Fadge

Serves 4

1 lb/455 g cooked potatoes

4 oz/113 g butter

4 oz/113 g all-purpose flour

1 tsp salt

1 large tart apple, peeled, cored, and grated or thinly sliced

A sprinkle of sugar

Mash the potatoes while they are still warm with the butter. Sift the flour and salt together and add to the potatoes. Form into a round and roll out on a floured work surface to a round about ¼ inch/6 mm thick.

Cover one side of the round with the apple and sprinkle with sugar. (The sweetness of the apple will determine the amount of sugar needed.) Then moisten the edges and fold over to seal the potato cake. Lightly grease a heavy frying pan and cook slowly on both sides over a medium heat so that the apple inside is cooked. Serve hot, spread with extra butter.

Kinky's Note:

I like to use Bramley apples grown in the beautiful orchards of Co Armagh. These are quite a tart apple and do need a little sugar.

Oven Soda Bread

Traditionally, soda bread was shaped into a round and placed into a greased iron pot called a Bastible. This looked rather like a Dutch oven and was hung over the fire in the hearth.

Makes 1
1 lb/455 g all-purpose flour
1 tsp baking soda
1 tsp salt
1 oz/28 g butter
20 oz/590 ml buttermilk

Preheat the oven to 425°F/220°C. Grease a 9 by 5-in (23 by 12-cm) loaf tin or a flat baking sheet.

Sift the flour, baking soda, and salt in a bowl and rub in the butter. Add the buttermilk and work gently but quickly into a soft dough. Place in the loaf tin or make into a round shape and place on the baking sheet. If you are making a round cake you need to mark a cross in the top to let the Devil out or to make it easier to cut into four segments. Bake for 20 to 30 minutes. The bread will sound hollow when the bottom is knocked. Turn the bread out onto a wire rack to cool and cover with a damp tea towel.

Kinky's Note:

Sometimes Ma would add currants or raisins just for a change. I loved this bread sliced and toasted (using a long-handled toasting fork shaped like a trident) in front of the fire and smothered with butter.

Ulster Buttermilk Scones

Makes 12 scones

8 oz/227 g all-purpose flour

2½ tsp baking powder

½ tsp baking soda

A pinch of salt

2 oz/56 g sugar

3 oz/85 g butter

1 egg, beaten, plus 1 egg yolk

4–5 Tbsp buttermilk

Milk

Preheat the oven to 400°F/200°C and line a large baking sheet with greased baking parchment.

Sift the flour, baking powder, baking soda, and salt into a bowl and add the sugar. Cut the butter into the flour and rub in with your fingers. Then stir in the egg and a tablespoon of buttermilk. Gradually work in the rest of the buttermilk to make a dough. (Different brands of flour may use more or less buttermilk, so do this slowly as you may have too much or you may need to add more.) When it all comes together in a soft dough, turn it out onto a floured work surface, knead it lightly, and roll it out to about 1 inch/2.5 cm or more thick. Now take a 1½-inch/4-cm cutter or a small upturned glass tumbler and cut out rounds.

Arrange the scones on the baking sheet and brush with a little egg yolk mixed with a little milk to give the scones a golden top (or you could simply dust them with flour). Bake for about 10 minutes until the tops have browned slightly and the scones have risen. Allow to cool on a wire rack.

I've
Half a
Mind to...

One of the first things my mentor taught me very early in our partnership was a rule taught to him by a Doctor Phelim Corrigan in 1936, in a dispensary practice in the Liberties in Dublin. "Never, never, never, let the patient get the upper hand." And as interpreted by O'Reilly, it did not apply only to patients.

He was no great respecter of titles or position when it came to appying that law. I recognised that from the morning when an overbearing patient, a local dignitary, who was dissatisfied with having to take his turn in the waiting room, demanded in a loud voice, "O'Reilly, do you know who I am?"

O'Reilly stopped, looked down on the seated man, cocked his head, and with a grin enquired of the packed waiting room, "Can anybody help? This gentleman seems to be suffering from amnesia. He's forgotten his own name."

The resultant gales of laughter weren't quite up to those Bob Hope or Jack Benny could command, but they didn't fall far short, either.

O'Reilly, while not averse to taking his time when it came to seeing patients—usually because he refused to rush anyone through their consultation—detested being kept waiting himself. I first noticed this on one of our trips to the Mucky Duck when Willie Dunleavy had been slower than usual in pouring O'Reilly's pint.

"Tell me Willie," O'Reilly leaned over the bar and asked in dulcet tones, "were you aware that under Brehon law, the statutes that governed Ireland from the dawn of time, the publican could be fined three sheep and a cow if anyone died of thirst in the public bar?"

Willie, suitably contrite, allowed that he wasn't, but on this occasion the doctor's pint was on the house. The upper hand definitely resided in O'Reilly's corner then too.

And it did when he was kept waiting by a very eminent colleague.

He had been invited to a meeting in the Royal Victoria Hospital in Belfast and had brought me along for moral support.

He parked the big Rover in the car park and we started walking to the hospital.

"I've to see the newly installed professor of what is now being called 'family medicine' instead of 'general practice.' Funny kind of term. 'Family medicine.'"

"What's in a name?" I said. "That which we call a rose by any other name would smell as sweet."

"Juliet. *Romeo and Juliet* act two, scene two," he remarked, "but honestly I never saw what we do at work as an academic specialty. Maybe I'm wrong."

Good Lord. O'Reilly wrong? More likely the Pope would be in error after having spoken *ex cathedra* . . . when supposedly he's infallible.

"Aye," said O'Reilly, "They've invited me up to discuss the possibility of our taking medical students into the practice so they can see what it's like in the trenches, not just look after the exotic cases that get sent to teaching hospitals."

I nodded, thinking of the first time I'd met Maggie MacCorkle. "Right enough," I said, "in all my four and a half years at the Royal Victoria, I never saw one patient with headaches two inches above the crown of her head. I think it's a great idea. Showing students what we actually do."

"And," he said, glancing at his watch, "we'd better get a move on. I don't want to be late for the meeting."

We lengthened our strides.

"Have they offered you any salary? Title?" I asked.

He nodded. "No money, but I'd get to be a clinical professor."

"And would you like that?" We had finished climbing the stairs in the Clinical Institute.

O'Reilly shook his head. "Not at all. I'd still be Fingal Flahertie O'Reilly, title or no title."

I did tell you right at the start he was no respecter of titles. I was soon to have that trait most convincingly reaffirmed.

He opened a door marked "DEPARTMENT OF FAMILY MEDICINE."

A woman, presumably the departmental secretary, sat behind her desk finishing writing something. Eventually she looked up at us over her spectacles. "Yes?" That one word held in its tones the contempt felt by important members of the medical establishment for pharmaceutical salesmen, mendicants, and the least of beings in the eyes of the hierarchy, medical students.

"Fingal O'Reilly to see John MacIlderry at twelve o'clock." He glanced at an inner door labelled PROFESSOR OF FAMILY MEDICINE, then looked at a wall mounted clock reading one minute to twelve. "He's a Trinity graduate like me. I know him."

"Have a seat," she said, indicating a couple of arm chairs behind a low table. "*Professor* MacIlderry is engaged." She went back to her writing.

O'Reilly shrugged and sat.

I merely sat.

"Tick." The minute hand registered twelve.

O'Reilly inhaled. Deeply.

"Tick." One minute past.

O'Reilly's next indrawing would have been described by Kinky as "strong enough to draw a shmall little cat up a chimney." I could tell he was not well pleased. O'Reilly's temper could always be judged by the depth of pallor on the tip of his bent nose. Then it was gently off-white.

By ten minutes past, with not as much as an "I'm sorry" from Cruella de Vil behind the desk, O'Reilly said sotto voce, "I know for a fact that Kinky's doing chicken with green peppercorns for lunch. She gets a bit upset if we're late and . . ." his tummy growled, "my belly thinks my throat's cut." He asked in his most dulcet tones, "Excuse me, but do you think the professor will be much long—"

"Professor MacIlderry is in an important meeting with Professor Scott of Social Medicine. You'll simply have to wait."

"Professor Scott is it? I know him, too."

I wondered what O'Reilly's knowing the two men in question had to do with anything and I was worrying about a possible eruption. I had read that escape of hydrogen from a tectonic fault line can predict an imminent massive earthquake. O'Reilly's nosetip had attained that shade of blue-white only seen on Antarctic icebergs. Any minute now . . . But to my surprise he rose and asked mildly, "May I borrow a sheet of paper and two drawing pins?"

I frowned. What for?

"Thank you," he said.

I watched as he printed something in block letters on the paper, moved to the door to the inner office, and pinned what he had written on the door. I couldn't see because he turned to the secretary and his body obscured the door. "We'll be leaving now," he said. "Please give my apologies to John." With that he stepped away from the door.

As I rose to join him I saw he had written in block capitals "DO NOT DISTURB. GREAT MIND AT WORK."

"Don't you mean minds?" I asked.

He turned and looked the secretary right in the eye. "I've known John MacIlderry and Roddy Scott for thirty years. 'Great mind' is accurate." He paused for a long while, then said, his voice cutting as a Wilkinson's Sword razor blade, "Both of them are only halfwits to begin with so 'great mind,' singular, is probably being overly generous." And with that he stormed out into the hall, with me trailing in his wake.

Two days later he received a written apology from Professor

MacIlderry and an invitation to dinner at the faculty club to discuss their business.

I think my old mentor kept the upper hand—and with a man of title, too.

MAINS

Traditional Ulster Fry

The Ulster fry dates back to Victorian times and the English version was included in *Mrs. Beeton's Book of Household Management*. An Ulster fry was usually eaten at breakfast time and was regarded as the best meal to set you up for a hard day's work or for play. There was also a belief that it was a good cure for a hangover. In Ulster most restaurants and pubs now serve the Ulster fry at any time of the day.

Black pudding is usually included in an Ulster fry and is made from pork blood, oatmeal, pork fat, spices, and onion, encased in a sausage skin. It is an acquired taste and some people prefer white pudding, which is similar but does not contain blood. White pudding , however, is not traditionally part of an Ulster Fry.

Regional variations are known as a Full English, a Full Scottish, or a Full Irish and there are differences between them. The English and Scottish breakfasts will include baked beans and sometimes mushrooms. The Full Irish includes white pudding.

Serves 1
Canola oil (about 2 Tbls or more if you need it)
2 pork sausages (Cookstown if you can get them)
2 slices bacon
1 tomato
1 Soda Farl (page 89)
Irish Potato Bread (page 93)
Black pudding
2 eggs (free-range if available)

Turn the oven on at its lowest setting to warm the plates. Heat a little of the oil in a large frying pan over a low heat. Then prick the sausages with a fork and cook gently, turning occasionally, until they are just coloured. Add the bacon to the pan and fry until it becomes crispy but not burnt. Remove the sausages and bacon to a warm dish in the oven and cover with kitchen paper.

Slice the tomato in half and place in the pan. Cut the soda farl in half and fry in the residue of the bacon fat. Add the potato bread and continue cooking for just long enough for the potato bread to brown on the outside and stay soft in the middle and the soda farl to absorb the delicious bacon flavour. Remove to the oven to keep warm. Slice the black pudding. Fry quickly and place in the oven.

Clean the pan with a quick wipe of paper towels. Put the remaining oil in the pan. Crack the eggs into the pan and add a teaspoon of water, then cover the pan. The water will create steam and cook the top of the egg. Before you know it, the eggs will be ready by the time you have plated the rest of the Ulster Fry onto a clean warm plate. Serve.

Kinky's Eggs Benedict
with Soda Farls

Serves 4

2 Soda Farls (Page 89)

4 slices bacon

4 fresh eggs

Hollandaise Sauce

3 eggs

2 Tbsp white wine vinegar

1 Tbsp lemon juice

Salt and freshly ground black pepper

4 oz/113 g butter

Boiling water

Make the soda farls first. You can have these ready in the freezer to use at any time. You will need only half a farl per person unless of course you are giving everyone 2 eggs each.

Grill or fry the bacon and keep warm.

Now make the Hollandaise Sauce.

I do this in a blender but you may want to use a whisk. Separate the egg yolks and egg whites.

Heat the vinegar and lemon juice in a small saucepan and reduce to about half. Put the vinegar mixture into the blender and gradually add the egg yolks and salt and pepper with the blender running slowly. Melt the butter in the same pan that you used for the vinegar and with the blender still running add the melted butter to the egg yolk mixture. The sauce will start to thicken and if you think it is too thick just add a little hot water.

What you have now is a traditional Hollandaise Sauce. I like to make more than I need so that I always have some in the freezer and am prepared to make a quick Benedict. However, the traditional Hollandaise does not freeze at all, so what you have to do is to beat up your leftover egg whites until they form soft peaks and fold them into the Hollandaise mixture. Freeze in individual portions and when needed just thaw and heat gently in a bain-marie or in a microwave on very low power for just a few seconds.

Poached Egg
1 egg per person
1 Tbsp vinegar
Boiling water

For a soft poached egg, bring a pan of water to the boil, then add the vinegar and reduce to a gentle simmer. Crack the egg into a bowl. Using a spoon, swirl the water in the pan to create a whirlpool, then carefully pour the egg into the centre of the whirlpool. Poach for 2 minutes, or until the whites are just set, then remove and place in a bowl of iced water until you are ready to use. To reheat the eggs just put into hot water for a few seconds and drain with a slotted spoon and a paper towel.

To assemble the Eggs Benedict
Cut the farls in half and toast and butter them. Place the grilled bacon on top, then the lightly poached egg. Finally pour the Hollandaise sauce over the top and serve straight away.

Beef

Beef Wellington

Serves 6

DUXELLES

A splash of truffle oil or olive oil

3 shallots, finely chopped

1 garlic clove, crushed

1 lb/455 g cremini or chestnut mushrooms, chopped

1 Tbsp finely chopped fresh parsley

BEEF AND PASTRY

2¼ lb/1 kg fillet of beef, trimmed

1 small bunch fresh thyme leaves

Sea salt and freshly ground black pepper

1 Tbsp olive oil

2 Tbsp strong English mustard or prepared horseradish

1 package frozen puff pastry, about 1 lb/455 g, thawed

1 egg, beaten

Coarse sea salt

FOR THE DUXELLES:

Heat the oil in a large frying pan over a medium-high heat, add the shallots and garlic, then add the mushrooms and cook until all the moisture from the mushrooms has evaporated. Add the chopped parsley.

FOR THE BEEF AND PASTRY:

Dry the fillet of beef with a paper towel, use a sharp knife to make a crisscross diamond pattern on the surface, and sprinkle with the thyme, plenty of salt, and pepper. In a large frying pan heat the oil over a high heat and sear the beef on all sides and each end. Now spread mustard over the entire fillet, wrap in cling film, and leave to chill in a refrigerator. (This may be done up to 24 hours ahead.)

When you are ready to cook the beef preheat the oven to 450°F/220°C. Roll out the puff pastry to a size that will completely wrap around the beef plus an extra inch or two for sealing. Spread the duxelles over the pastry. Lay the beef on top, then fold the pastry round it and moisten and seal the pastry edges. Brush the pastry with the beaten egg and use a sharp knife to make a crisscross pattern. Sprinkle the pastry with some coarse sea salt to help it to crisp. Bake for 30 to 35 minutes, until the pastry is crisp and golden, then remove from the oven and allow to rest for 10 to 12 minutes. Using a really sharp knife, cut into slices and serve.

Kinky's Note:

When I made this for the marquis I added another step to the recipe but it really makes the dish much richer and is probably more suited to a very grand occasion, so. What you need is a portion of pâté de foie gras, a tablespoon of brandy, and some very thin pancakes or crêpes. You put a layer of pâté, softened with the brandy, onto the pancakes and place this, pâté side up, between the pastry and the duxelles.

VARIATION

Venison Wellington. Replace the beef with a boned loin of venison and proceed as before.

Beef and Dumplings

Serves 6

BEEF STEW

4–5 lb/1.8–2.3 kg bone-in brisket

25 oz/740 ml beef stock

8 oz/235 ml red wine

2 onions, chopped

3 or 4 carrots, peeled and chopped

2 Tbsp tomato puree

2 Tbsp fresh thyme leaves

1 Tbsp whole black peppercorns

4 bay leaves

Salt and freshly ground black pepper

1 bunch fresh parsley, chopped

SUET DUMPLINGS

14 oz/400 g self-rising flour

2 Tbsp chopped fresh parsley, plus extra for sprinkling

2 tsp salt

7 oz/200 g suet

Water

FOR THE BEEF STEW:

Preheat the oven to 225°F/100°C. Put the brisket in a Dutch oven or lidded casserole dish and add the stock, wine, onions, carrots, tomato puree, thyme, peppercorns, and bay leaves. Cover the pot with foil and then the lid. You want this to be a really tight fit so that it will not evaporate too much. Cook for about 8 hours or overnight. (Alternatively, you could use a slow cooker.)

Allow the beef to cool in the cooking liquid then remove and slice into portions and set aside. Remove the bay leaves. Before you skim the surface fat from the liquor it helps to chill it in the refrigerator first.

So skim off the fat and liquidise the stock, adjust the salt and freshly ground black pepper, and bring up to a simmer on the stovetop. If the stock seems a little watery, just turn up the heat and reduce the quantity. Return the beef to the cooking pot together with the chopped parsley.

FOR THE SUET DUMPLINGS:

Combine the flour, parsley, and salt in a bowl and rub or cut the suet in. Add water to make a dough. Form the dough into egg-shaped pieces and add to the meat and the stock. Cover and simmer for about 15 minutes, by which time the dumplings will have doubled in size. Serve in individual dishes with some chopped parsley sprinkled over.

Kinky's Note:

For really light dumplings do not open the lid when cooking, and keep it just at a simmer.

BEEF COBBLER

Instead of suet dumplings you could try this scone topping for a nice change.

COBBLER SCONE TOPPING
3½ oz/100 g whole-wheat flour
3½ oz/100 g all-purpose flour

1 Tbsp finely chopped fresh rosemary

2 tsp baking powder

½ tsp baking soda

A pinch of salt

5½ oz/156 g cheddar cheese, grated

4 to 5 Tbsp buttermilk

1 egg, beaten

Chopped fresh parsley

Preheat the oven to 425°F/220°C.

Whisk together the whole-wheat flour, all-purpose flour, rosemary, baking powder, baking soda, and salt in a bowl and stir in all but a couple of tablespoons of the cheese. Stir in the buttermilk gradually to make a soft dough. (You may not need all the milk or you may need a little more.)

Turn the dough out onto a floured work surface and, working quickly, roll out to about 1 inch thick. Cut out round scones, glaze with beaten egg, and top with the reserved cheese, pressing it down a little so that it sticks to the top of the scones. Now place these on the surface of the beef stew in the casserole and bake uncovered for 25 minutes or until the scone topping has risen and is golden brown. Sprinkle with chopped parsley and serve.

Beef and Guinness Stew

Serves 4

2 Tbsp all-purpose flour

Salt and freshly ground black pepper

1 lb 2 oz/500 g stewing steak, cut in 2-in/5-cm chunks

2 Tbsp canola oil, plus extra as needed

2 large onions, chopped

2 large carrots, peeled and chopped

1 parsnip, peeled and chopped

8 oz/235 ml Guinness

34 oz/1 L beef stock

1 small bunch fresh thyme

Season the flour well with salt and pepper and coat the steak with the seasoned flour. Heat the oil in a Dutch oven or pan with a lid over a medium to hot heat. Gradually add the meat to the hot oil and brown on all sides. Don't add too much at a time. When all the meat has been browned, remove it from the Dutch oven to a plate. Now add the onions, carrots, and parsnip and a little more oil if necessary. Don't worry about the brown caramelised remains of the meat as this all adds to the flavour. Stir the vegetables around for a few minutes and then return the meat to the pan.

Add the Guinness and cook, stirring to scrape the remains from the bottom. Add the stock and the thyme and allow to simmer slowly for 2 or 3 hours. Remove the lid and the thyme stalks and cook for a further 30 minutes or so until the liquid has reduced by about half. Serve with Champ (page 209) and suet dumplings or scone cobbler on top.

Kinky's Note:

I like to make the stew the previous day because I think this improves the flavour. Then when you cook it the following day you can make the suet dumplings or cobbler topping to finish it off.

Corned Beef Curry

Patrick Taylor's father, Squadron Leader Jimmy Taylor, RAFVR, had been stationed in Basra during the Second World War. An Indian regiment was part of the garrison and the officers' messes entertained each other. While the Hindu soldiers were vegetarian and ate vegetarian curries, the RAF cookhouse had created one using corned beef as yet another way to serve the tinned meat, which was in plentiful supply (whereas fresh meat often was not). Jimmy was so impressed with the dish that he obtained the recipe and it was a popular meal at home after the war when Patrick Taylor was a boy.

Serves 4

1 Tbsp vegetable oil or olive oil

1 onion, chopped

2 carrots, peeled and finely chopped

1 potato or small turnip, diced

4 garlic cloves, crushed

1 (1-in/2.5-cm) piece fresh ginger, grated

1 red chile, seeded and chopped

½ small green chile, seeded and chopped

1 tsp ground coriander

1 tsp ground cumin

1 tsp garam masala

Freshly ground black pepper

17 oz/505 ml vegetable stock

1 (14.5-oz/411-g) can diced tomatoes

½ cup (4 oz/113 g) raisins

1 (12-oz 340-g) can corned beef, cut into cubes

1 cup (8 oz/225 g) pineapple chunks

4 oz/113 g sour cream

2 Tbsp chopped fresh cilantro

Heat the oil in a large frying pan over a low heat. Cover with a piece of parchment paper and the pan lid and gently sweat the onions, carrots, and potato in the hot oil for 5 minutes. Discard the parchment paper. Add the garlic, ginger, chilis, and spices, then the stock, tomatoes, and raisins. Cook for about 20 minutes, then add the corned beef and finish by stirring in the pineapple chunks, sour cream, and cilantro. Serve with cooked rice.

Cottage Pie
with Champ Topping

I am forever being asked what the difference is between cottage pie and shepherd's pie and the answer is that you use lamb instead of beef to make a shepherd's. This is very good, too, and reminds me so much of my childhood and a man called Connor MacTaggart, but you'll have to read *An Irish Country Girl* to find out why.

Serves 4 to 6

1 Tbsp cooking oil

2 onions, chopped

1 large or 2 small carrots, peeled and grated

1 lb/455 g lean ground beef

1 Tbsp chopped fresh parsley

1 Tbsp tomato puree or ketchup

1 Tbsp Worcestershire sauce

1 Tbsp all-purpose flour

Salt and freshly ground black pepper

10 oz/295 ml beef stock

Champ (page 209)

Butter

Cheddar cheese, grated

Preheat the oven to 400°F/200°C. Fry the onions and carrot in the oil in a large pan over a low to medium heat, stirring occasionally, for a few minutes. Add the beef and cook for a further 20 to 30 minutes. The beef will be nice and brown now and will have released its fat. To make this pie less fattening for himself, and so that Alice Malony, the local dressmaker, does not be having to let his waistband out some more, I like to press the beef mixture into a sieve and let most of the fat run through. Return the beef to the pan and add the parsley, tomato puree, Worcestershire sauce, flour, salt and pepper to taste, and finally the beef stock. Now simmer it all for a few minutes and adjust the seasoning if necessary.

Pour into a well-greased 7 by 7-inch baking dish. Spread the champ topping over the top of the cooked beef mixture, dot the top with butter and cheese, and bake for about 25 minutes. The topping will have browned nicely. Serve.

Homity Pie

This recipe was given to me by Doctor O'Reilly when he came back from the war. He said that Marge Wilcoxson, who was the wife of his senior officer on HMS *Warspite* and who lived in Fareham near the hospital in Gosport where O'Reilly had been seconded for training in anaesthesia, used to make it. It was invented by the Land Girls using ingredients they could grow in the fields. The Land Girls was the nickname given to the Women's Land Army set up in the first two world wars to recruit women to work on farms where men had left to go to war. This makes a substantial pie and would feed about six people.

Serves 6

PASTRY

4 oz/113 g butter

6½ oz/184 g all-purpose flour

¼ tsp cayenne pepper

A pinch of salt

A pinch of baking powder

3 oz/85 g strong cheddar cheese, grated

2½ Tbsp ice water

1½ Tbsp cider vinegar

FILLING

1¾ lb/800 g potatoes, peeled and cut into quarters

1 oz/28 g butter

1 Tbsp sunflower oil

3 onions, chopped

2 garlic cloves, crushed

6 oz/170 g strong cheddar cheese, coarsely grated

4 oz/113 g shredded spinach or broccoli florets

2 Tbsp chopped fresh parsley

Salt and freshly ground black pepper

A pinch of ground nutmeg

8 oz/235 ml heavy cream

FOR THE PASTRY:

Cut the butter into ¾-inch/2-cm cubes. Put in a plastic bag and freeze until solid. Place the flour, cayenne, salt, and baking powder in another plastic bag and freeze for at least a half hour.

Place the flour mixture in a food processor and process for a few seconds to combine. Add the cheese and pulse a few times. Now add the butter and pulse until the butter cubes are as small as peas. The mixture will be in loose particles. Add the water and vinegar and pulse briefly. Spoon it all back into the plastic bag. Hold the open end of the bag closed and knead the mixture with your other hand until it all holds together in one piece and feels stretchy when pulled. Remove the dough from the plastic bag and wrap it in plastic wrap and refrigerate for at least 45 minutes (but it will be better if you can leave it overnight).

Roll out the dough on a lightly floured surface. Line a deep 8-inch/20-cm pie dish with the pastry and crimp the edges. Leave covered in the refrigerator until needed (or see note page 129).

FOR THE FILLING:

Preheat the oven to 350°F/180°C. Cook the potatoes in boiling water for 15 minutes or until just tender. Drain and slice them and set aside to cool. Meanwhile, melt the butter and oil in a frying pan over a low heat, add the onions, and fry until soft and golden. Add the garlic and cook gently for a couple of minutes, being careful not to let it burn. Add the onions and garlic, half of the cheese, the spinach, parsley, nutmeg, and salt and pepper to taste to the potatoes and mix everything together well. Allow to cool.

Fill the pastry-lined tin with the vegetable and cheese mixture. Pour the cream over and sprinkle the remaining cheese on top. Place the tin on a baking sheet and bake for 40 to 45 minutes. Allow it to cool for about 5 minutes before cutting into thick wedges. As this is quite a filling pie it would be best to serve with a salad.

Kinky's Note:

If you want to ensure that the pie base will be crisp, you can partially prebake it. Just prick the pastry all over with a fork, line with parchment paper and baking beans, and bake blind for about 15 minutes.

Steak and Kidney Pudding

Serves 6

SUET PASTRY

14 oz/400 g self-rising flour

½ tsp salt

Freshly ground black pepper

7 oz/200 g beef suet or vegetarian suet

10 oz/295 ml cold water

FILLING

8 oz/227 g ox kidneys or lamb's kidneys

2 Tbsp all-purpose flour

Salt and freshly ground black pepper

1½ lb/680 g chuck steak, trimmed and cut into ¾-in/2-cm cubes

1 small onion, chopped

5 oz/150 ml beef stock

FOR THE PASTRY:

Sift the flour together with the salt and season with black pepper. Then add the suet and mix it in with a knife. It should appear as pea-size lumps. Gradually add the water until you have a stiff dough-like consistency. (Indeed you may need to use extra water, as some flour needs more than others.) Now with your hands, work it 'til you have a nice smooth dough. Roll about three-quarters of the dough out and fit it into a buttered pudding bowl about 1.5 L capacity.

FOR THE FILLING:

Prepare the kidneys by removing the outer membrane and cutting away all tubes and fat or gristle, then cut into ½-inch/12-cm pieces. Season the flour with salt and pepper in a large bowl. Add the steak and kidneys and toss to coat, then add the onion. Place the mixture in the pastry-lined pudding bowl and add enough beef stock to almost cover the meat. Now roll out the rest of the dough to make a lid, dampen the edges with water to make a good seal, and cover the pudding bowl with the dough. Cover the pudding with a double piece of buttered parchment with a pleat in the middle to allow for expansion. I use parchment paper, then foil tied on with string.

Once the string has been tied round the top of the bowl, tie the long end of the string to the opposite side of the bowl, making a loop to use as a handle. Set the bowl in a steamer or in a saucepan that you've lined with a trivet or an upturned plate. Add enough water to come halfway up the side of the bowl and steam over a moderate heat for about 5 hours. (You will have to remember to keep topping this up with water or it will boil dry.) To serve, turn the pudding out on a plate and cut into wedges. I like to accompany this with peas and mashed potatoes.

Steak and Kidney Pie

I think this is easier and quicker than the Steak and Kidney Pudding recipe (page 130) and it is also good served with mashed potatoes.

Serves 4

2 lamb's kidneys

1 lb/455 g stewing beef, trimmed and cut into 1-in/2.5-cm pieces

2 Tbsp all-purpose flour

2 Tbsp vegetable oil

2 onions, chopped

30 oz/885 ml beef stock, plus extra as needed

1 Tbsp Worcestershire sauce

Salt and freshly ground black pepper

1 package frozen puff pastry, about 1 lb/455 g, thawed, or Quick Flaky Pastry
  (recipe follows)

1 egg yolk and a little milk to glaze

Prepare the kidneys by removing the outer membrane and cutting away all tubes and fat or gristle, then slice into ⅜-inch/1-cm pieces. Dust the beef in the flour. Heat the oil in a large frying pan over a medium heat. Add the beef in several batches and brown it on all sides in the hot oil. (If you add it all at once it will not brown.) Add the kidneys and fry for 2 or 3 minutes.

Remove from the pan and fry the onions for a few minutes. Now return the meat and kidneys to the pan, sprinkle the remaining flour on top, add the beef stock and Worcestershire sauce, and simmer gently, covered, for 1½ hours. You want the gravy to reduce and thicken but watch that it does not all disappear. If it reduces too much just add some more stock. Now test for tenderness and season with salt and pepper to taste.

Preheat the oven to 425°F/220°C. Place the steak and kidney mixture in a 7-inch pie dish and allow it to cool. Roll out the pastry to a shape that will cover the filling and crimp round the edges; trim off the surplus. Brush with the egg and milk mixture and make a cut in the centre of the lid to allow the steam to escape. Bake for 30 to 40 minutes or until the pastry is risen and golden brown.

Kinky's Note:

When you need to coat meat in flour it is easy to do this in a plastic bag. Just put the flour in the bag, add the meat, close the top, and give it a good shake around.

Quick Flaky Pastry

If you prefer to make your own pastry, here is one that I like to do.

Makes 1 pie case or 1 pie top about 7 inches/18 cm in diameter
4 oz/113 g lard or margarine
6½ oz/184 all-purpose flour
½ tsp salt
A pinch of baking powder
4 tsp cider vinegar
2 oz/60 ml ice water

Chill the fat in the freezer for several hours. In a large bowl combine the flour, salt, and baking powder. Chop the lard or grate it using a coarse cheese grater, and mix it into the flour (or you can briefly process it in a food processor). Mix the vinegar and a little water together and stir into the flour. Don't add too much water to begin with, as you can add more later, if needed. Rest the pastry, wrapped in cling film, in the refrigerator for about 1 hour before rolling out. Then roll out on a very well-floured work surface and chill in the refrigerator until needed.

Kinky's Note:

1. If you use whole-wheat flour for the rolling out, it adds a nice, crunchy texture to the pastry.
2. If you are blind-baking a pie shell I think it is preferable to use a metal pie tin, as it gives a crisper finish than baking in a ceramic or glass dish. You can always transfer it to a ceramic or glass dish when adding the filling.

VARIATION

Steak and Mushroom Pie. Make as for Steak and Kidney Pie above but substitute 8 oz/227 g mushrooms for the lamb's kidneys.

Grave,
Where Is
Thy Victory?

"Will the defendant rise and face the bench," said the clerk of the magistrate's court on a Friday in October 1964. "His honour will pronounce his verdict."

O'Reilly stood.

It may be hard to believe, but he was here on a charge of poaching, a crime that not so very long ago had had a great deal to do with the populating of Botany Bay, Australia, by the transported guilty from Ireland. Taking a wild duck or goose out of season or nicking one of the local squire's game birds or rabbits or salmon or trout and getting caught usually resulted in a long, relaxing sea voyage at His Majesty King George III's expense to, and a prolonged tropical vacation in, *Terra Australis,* which was just then becoming a bit more *cognita*. A good row and a ruction, on the other hand, with black eyes and broken bones, which today would lead to charges of grievous bodily harm, was simply regarded as one of Ireland's national pastimes.

The present alleged (at least until judgement was passed) offence under consideration had occurred several months ago, shortly after I'd joined his practice. O'Reilly, who I later learned was usually meticulous in observing the dates of shooting seasons, had had a great hankering for wild duck roasted as only Kinky could. He'd reasoned that Stranford Lough was a lonely place and no one would see the dirty deed.

On his way home O'Reilly had dropped into the pub for a jar, and regrettably the long arm of the law had noticed the late bird's tail feathers sticking out of O'Reilly's coat pocket. With some profession of regret, Constable Mulligan had issued a summons to appear in front of the Ballybucklebo and townland resident magistrate, Mister Albert Cholmondely (pronounced Chumley), LL.B., solicitor at law, at the next magistrates' court.

O'Reilly'd asked me to keep him company at his short trial. He and I had sat on hard wooden chairs in the front row while Constable Mulligan, with several apologetic glances at O'Reilly, presented his evidence and was excused. Because of the eminence of the accused most of the local folks who were not at their work were crammed into the little courthouse.

From a raised dais, the magistrate looked down his angular nose and over half-moon spectacles at O'Reilly standing in front of his chair. Mister Cholmondely spoke in a high-pitched voice that sounded as if it was so raspy because someone had used sandpaper on his vocal cords: "In the matter of *Regina Versus O'Reilly* before this court, the matter of taking by shooting for the purpose of capturing, keeping, and retaining for possible resale or personal use one member of the sub-family genus *Anas* species *platyrhinchos* at a time outwith those months when the taking of the aforementioned birds is legally permitted, henceforth to be known as the 'shooting season,' in contravention of the *Game Act of Great Britain and Northern Ireland, 1831,* this court finds on the evidence presented the defendant, one Doctor Fingal Flahertie O'Reilly, medical practitioner of this village and townland, guilty as charged."

Any pins dropping would have dwarfed the row of the explosion of Krakatoa, so deep was the silence in the room.

I watched the defendant's bent nose turn pallid, a sure sign that he was enraged, and could tell he was becoming impatient because I could hear O'Reilly muttering under his breath, "For the sake of the wee man, get on with it."

Mister Cholmondely clearly relished his power over the defendant and, I surmised, was enjoying humbling such a locally important figure. The legal eagle probably thought he was a direct descendant of Judge Jeffreys, chief justice of the Bloody Assizes in 1685. Cholmondely probably regretted that he could not, like his forebear, sentence O'Reilly to hanging, drawing, and quartering. The RM said, waving a bony admonitory index finger, "Before passing sentence I wish to remind you, Doctor, of your position in the community. Yet instead of being the soul of righteousness, an example to all, you have sunk to the depths of a common criminal. You should be ashamed of yourself, sir. Ashamed."

O'Reilly was managing to look contrite, but I could see the fires of the inferno in the depths of his brown eyes.

"For any ordinary citizen I would have levied a fine of five guineas. In your case, Doctor . . ." he said the word with an inflection he might have used in sentencing a mass murderer. "In your case you will pay to the clerk of this court the sum of fifteen guineas."

From behind came a chorus of gasps and sighs.

"Case dismissed." He banged his gavel and sneered at O'Reilly.

O'Reilly dutifully coughed up the money and nodded at the little crowd of onlookers as we left. On our way home from the courthouse he said, "I don't mind being fined. It was wrong to shoot out of season and stupid to get caught, but nobody and I mean nobody preaches at me like that in front of my patients. Half of getting them better depends on how much faith they have in their doctor. That faith was rocked today."

"I don't know, Fingal," I said. "I thought there was fair bit of sympathy for you in there."

"Maybe." O'Reilly grunted and then said, "I wonder how he'd like to be humbled in his own courthouse?"

I confess that the entire matter slipped my mind until summer rolled around and O'Reilly said, as we were taking a pre-prandial and nibbling on gravadlax on Guinness bread in his upstairs lounge, "The next magistrate's court will be held tomorrow and I have a petition before it. My brother Lars the solicitor helped me with the preparation. Want to come along?"

Then I remembered O'Reilly's exact words after his last encounter with the RM: "I wonder how he'd like to be humbled in his own courthouse?" Nothing short of a small nuclear explosion would have kept me away.

"I just need to tell you something in advance," he said.

"Fire away," I said, sipping my sherry.

"I have," he said, "recently been examining old gravestones. Sonny Houston has been helping me. You know he's interested in archaelogy."

"I didn't," I said, remembering the strange old gentleman who, because of a row with a certain Councillor Bertie Bishop over an unfinished roof, had once lived in his car. And what the blazes could his helping O'Reilly with gravestones have to do with humbling an RM?

I found out the next morning.

Once more the courtroom was packed and Mister Albert Cholmondely sat enthroned above the common herd, the might and panoply of *Lex Brittanica* personified—at least, I thought, in his own mind.

The clerk of the court announced, "The next case is a petiton by Doctor O'Reilly for an exhumation. Will the petitioner rise?"

O'Reilly did so from his seat in the front row offset to one side so he half-faced the bench and half-faced the audience.

There was a mumbling throughout the room.

O'Reilly said, "Your honour, may it please the court, in my position of local medical examiner I wish to apply under the *United Kingdom's Burial Act of 1857,* which among other things covers exhumations . . ."

"Do not, Doctor, try to teach your granny to suck eggs," the RM said. "I am perfectly familiar with the relevant section. Please proceed and do not be wasting this court's time."

O'Reilly produced a sheet of paper that was covered in blacking which must have been applied as the sheet lay over a tombstone. Like a brass rubbing, the inscription had been highlighted. "Will your honour please read this?"

"Give it here." The paper was accepted and Mister Cholmondely began to read aloud. "R.I.P Eamonn McCann 1784–1836. Here lies a Resident Magistrate and an honest man." Cholmondely whipped off his spectacles. "I fail to see the relevance of this to an application to dig up the grave. Explain yourself, O'Reilly."

O'Reilly shook his head and said, looking the RM straight in the eye, "Please forgive me, your honour, but you've just told me that you are, may I quote you, 'perfectly familiar with the relevant section.'"

A subdued murmuring filled the room.

The RM spluttered, banged his gavel, and shouted, "Silence in court. Silence in court."

The murmuring subsided, but before the RM could speak O'Reilly faced the crowd and, holding open a legal tome and pointing at the page, said, "The inscription your honour just read says 'an RM and an honest man,' and under the act, may I quote? 'It is strictly prohibited to bury two people in one grave.'"

Silence for a moment, then the meaning sank in and the eruption of laughter, cat calls, and stamping of boots on the wooden floor probably stopped the RM hearing O'Reilly, who bent low and stretched out both arms sideways as he said in his best TV lawyer, Perry Mason's manner, "Your honour, I rest my case."

Chicken
AND
Duck

Irish Country Chicken Breasts

Serves 4

4 boneless, skinless chicken breasts

Salt

1 oz/28 g butter

1 cup fresh white bread crumbs (crusts removed from the bread)

2½ oz/75 ml white wine

Juice of ½ lemon

8 oz/235 ml heavy cream

3 egg yolks

Freshly ground black pepper

2½ oz/70 g cheddar cheese, grated

Preheat the oven to 400°F/200°C. Sprinkle the chicken breasts with salt. Melt the butter in a large frying pan over a medium heat, add the chicken breasts, and cook for 10 to 15 minutes, until just lightly coloured on both sides. Put them, arranged side by side, in a greased ovenproof dish. In the butter remaining in the pan, cook the bread crumbs until they are golden but not too brown. Set to one side and deglaze the pan with the white wine and the lemon juice until it has reduced to about half its volume. Leave in the pan until you are ready to use it.

Beat the cream and egg yolks in a bowl, season with salt and pepper, and stir in the cheese. Pour the deglazing liquid from the pan over the chicken breasts, followed by the cream mixture and finish by sprinkling the golden crumbs over the top. Bake for about 25 minutes, until the top is golden brown and the egg mixture is firm. Serve with new potatoes and green peas or beans.

Chicken with Green Peppercorns

Serves 4

4 boneless, skinless chicken breasts

2 oz/56 g butter

2 shallots, chopped

2 Tbsp Worcestershire sauce

2 garlic cloves, crushed

1 tsp whole green peppercorns

2 oz/60 ml brandy

2 oz/60 ml strong chicken stock

4 oz/120 ml heavy cream

Salt

Put the chicken breasts between two pieces of waxed paper and pound with a rolling pin until they are of an even thickness of about ½ inch. Melt the butter in a large frying pan over a medium heat. Add the shallots and fry gently for 2 to 3 minutes. Then add the chicken breasts and cook on each side for about 8 minutes, until just cooked through and lightly browned. Remove from the pan to a serving dish large enough to accommodate the breasts. Add the Worcestershire sauce, garlic, and peppercorns to the pan. Mash the peppercorns with a fork and add the brandy and chicken stock. Cook over a high heat for a minute or two until the liquid is reduced and the pan is deglazed. Reduce the heat, stir in the cream, and cook, stirring all the time until the cream begins to thicken. Season with salt to taste and pour this over the chicken and heat through in the oven. Keep covered in a warm oven until you are ready to serve it. Delicious served with rice, Champ (page 209), or new potatoes.

Lemony Chicken
with Mustard Sauce

Serves 4

1 Tbsp sunflower or canola oil

4 boneless, skinless chicken breasts

10½ oz/310 ml chicken stock

A knob of butter

2 Tbsp Dijon mustard

1 tsp chopped fresh tarragon

Grated zest of 1 lemon plus ½ large lemon, sliced (or slice a whole lemon
   if small)

½ tsp salt

Freshly ground black pepper

8 oz/235 ml heavy cream

2 oz/60 ml dry white wine

Lemon Rice (Page 214)

Heat the oil in a large frying pan over a medium heat, add the chicken, and cook until browned. Pour the chicken stock over the chicken breasts and add the butter, mustard, tarragon, lemon zest, salt, and pepper. Cover and simmer gently for 30 minutes. Remove the chicken to a serving dish and keep warm. Now add the cream and wine to the pan and boil up to thicken the sauce and reduce it by about a third. Add the lemon slices and simmer gently for a further 5 minutes. Adjust the seasoning if necessary. Pour the sauce over the chicken and serve with lemon rice.

Pan-Seared Duck Breasts
with Port and Redcurrant Sauce

Serves 4

4 8-oz/227-g duck breasts, skin on

3 shallots, finely chopped

3 oz/85 g butter, cubed

8 oz/235 ml chicken stock

6 oz/170 g redcurrants

6 oz/180 ml port or red wine

1 tsp brown sugar (optional)

Salt and freshly ground black pepper

Dry each breast with a paper towel and use a sharp knife to make a crisscross diamond pattern on the skin. Place the duck breasts into a cold, dry frying pan. (Do not add any oil or butter.) Turn up the heat and cook skin-side down until the skin becomes quite crispy and the fat has been released.

Now before you cook the other side you may need to pour off most of the fat first. Reserve this fat for later and cook the breasts for a very short time, say 3 to 4 minutes if you like it pink in the middle. Leave the breasts uncovered for 5 minutes before removing to a cutting board and slicing each one diagonally against the grain.

Gently cook the shallots in the residue in the pan without allowing them to burn. You may need to add a knob of butter. Add the chicken stock and redcurrants and cook until the fruit is soft. Pour and push the sauce through a fine-mesh sieve into a clean pan, add the port, and bring to a brisk boil. Reduce the liquid by almost half and whisk in the remaining butter. Add the sugar and season with salt and pepper to taste. Serve the duck with the sauce on the side and Himmel und Urde (page 213) or simple Champ (page 209).

Keep the reserved fat refrigerated in a covered container to roast potatoes at another time.

VARIATION

Pan-Seared Duck Breasts with Rhubarb Sauce. Simmer 5 chopped rhubarb stalks, 2 tablespoons brown sugar, and 2 to 3 tablespoons water together until the rhubarb becomes soft. Allow to cool slightly and process in a blender. Serve this with the cooked duck instead of the port and redcurrant sauce. (Rhubarb sauce is also delicious with oily fish such as mackerel or with pork, instead of applesauce.)

Parmesan Chicken

Serves 4

2 oz/56 g butter

4 boneless, skinless chicken breasts

4 oz/120 ml dry white wine

2 oz/60 ml sherry

Grated zest of 1 lemon, plus 4 oz/120 ml lemon juice and lemon slices for
  garnish

Grated zest of 1 orange, plus orange slices for garnish

10 oz/295 ml light cream

4 oz/113 g Parmesan cheese, grated

Melt the butter in a large frying pan over a medium heat, add the chicken breasts, and sauté until browned and cooked through. Remove the chicken to a heatproof serving dish. Add the wine, sherry, citrus zest, and lemon juice to the pan. Turn up the heat to reduce the liquid and deglaze the pan. Lower the heat and stir in the cream. Sprinkle the cheese over the chicken and brown under a grill or broiler. Pour the sauce over the chicken breasts and garnish with the lemon and orange slices. Serve with rice and a green salad.

Lamb

Irish Stew

Serves 4 to 6

2¼ lb/1 kg bone-in lamb neck

1 Tbsp cooking oil

101 oz/3 L water

Salt and freshly ground black pepper

1 bay leaf

5 floury potatoes, cut into quarters

2 onions, chopped small

4–5 carrots, peeled and chopped small

5 waxy potatoes, cut into quarters

Worcestershire sauce

Chopped fresh parsley

First, scrape as much meat off the bones as possible and put the meat to one side. Heat the oil in a large pot over a medium to high heat and brown the bones for a few minutes. Add the water, season with salt and pepper, add the bay leaf, and bring to the boil. Simmer gently for about 2 hours. By this time the liquid should have reduced down to about 1 quart/1 L. Leave it to get cold so that you can remove the fat from the surface. (Putting it in the fridge really helps to solidify the fat.)

Scrape any remaining meat from the bones again and discard the bones. Now add with the rest of the meat to the liquid and cook for about 30 minutes. Then add the floury potatoes, onions, and carrots and cook for another 10 or 15 minutes or so, by which time the potatoes will start to break up and thicken the cooking liquid. Add the waxy potatoes and cook for a further 20 minutes or so over a gentle heat, stirring occasionally. Season to taste and add a few drops of Worcestershire (or other spicy brown) sauce. Sprinkle with chopped parsley and serve.

Kinky's Note:

1. I like to make this over a period of two days as there can be quite a lot of fat to remove from the surface and it is much easier to do it after it has been refrigerated overnight and the fat has solidified.

2. The reason that I use both floury and waxy potatoes is that the floury ones help to thicken the cooking juices and the waxy ones retain their shape.

Braised Lamb Shanks

Lamb shanks can be from the shoulder or the hind leg. The shoulder takes longer to cook, so to achieve an even result cook the same types together. If possible, use a heavy-bottomed Dutch oven with a tight-fitting lid.

Serves 4

4 lamb shanks
Salt and freshly ground black pepper
2 Tbsp vegetable oil or olive oil
2 carrots, peeled and chopped
1 onion, chopped
2 celery stalks, chopped
10 garlic cloves
10 oz/295 ml red wine
10 oz/295 ml lamb or vegetable stock
1 Tbsp tomato puree
1 sprig fresh rosemary
1 sprig fresh thyme
2 bay leaves

Preheat the oven to 350°F/180°C. Season the shanks with salt and pepper.

Heat the oil in a large Dutch oven over a medium heat, add the shanks and brown them in the oil. Remove the lamb, add the carrots, onion, celery, and garlic and sauté for a few minutes. Pour in the red wine, bring to the boil, and simmer for a minute or two. Add the stock, tomato purée, rosemary, thyme, and bay leaves and place the shanks on top. Bring to the boil, cover, and cook in the oven for 1½ to 2½ hours, depending on the size and cut. (You can also do what I do and cook it on the stovetop if your pan is heavy-bottomed, but you will need to check the liquid level from time to time to make sure that it does not boil dry; add extra stock or water if the level looks too low.)

When the lamb has finished cooking, remove the shanks to a serving dish. Discard the herbs and half the vegetables. With an immersion blender, puree the remaining vegetables to thicken the sauce and, if necessary, reduce the remaining liquid in the casserole by bringing to the boil for a minute or two. There should only be just enough sauce to coat each lamb shank. Serve with Champ (page 209) and Redcurrant Jelly (page 242).

Lamb Wellington

Serves 4 to 6

DUXELLES

A splash of truffle oil

3 shallots, finely chopped

1 garlic clove, crushed

2 rosemary leaves finely chopped

1 lb/455 g cremini mushrooms, finely chopped

1 Tbsp fresh parsley, finely chopped

LAMB

2¼ lb/1 kg boned fillet of lamb or boneless lamb loin

1 small bunch fresh thyme leaves

Sea salt and freshly ground black pepper

1 package frozen puff pastry, about 1 lb/455 g, thawed

2 Tbsp Dijon mustard or prepared horseradish

1 egg

FOR THE DUXELLES:

Heat the oil in a large frying pan over a medium-high heat, add the shallots, garlic, and rosemary, then add the mushrooms and cook until all the moisture from the mushrooms has evaporated. Add the chopped parsley.

FOR THE LAMB:

Dry the lamb fillet with paper towels and sprinkle with the thyme, plenty of salt, and pepper. In a large frying pan, heat the oil over a high heat and sear the lamb on all sides and each end. Now spread mustard over the entire fillet, wrap in cling film, and leave to chill in a refrigerator. (This may be done up to 24 hours ahead.)

When you are ready to cook the lamb, preheat the oven to 450°F/220°C. Roll out the puff pastry to a size that will completely wrap around the lamb plus an extra inch or two for sealing. Spread the duxelles over the pastry. Lay the lamb on top, then fold the pastry round it and moisten and seal the pastry edges. Brush the pastry with the beaten egg and use a sharp knife to make a crisscross pattern. Sprinkle the pastry with some coarse sea salt to help it to crisp. Bake for 30 to 35 minutes, until the pastry is crisp and golden, then remove from the oven and allow to rest for 10 to 12 minutes. Using a really sharp knife, cut into slices. Serve with buttered garden peas, new baby potatoes, and Mint Chutney (page 205) or Mint Sauce (page 247).

Roast Rack of Lamb
with Caper Sauce

Himself thinks this is a grand feast altogether and likes me to serve it with buttery mashed potatoes and peas. Ask your butcher to French trim the lamb. There will probably be eight ribs in each rack.

Serves 4 to 6

2 racks of lamb, trimmed

Salt and freshly ground black pepper

A knob of butter

1 Tbsp sunflower or canola oil

2 tsp Dijon mustard

4 oz/113 g fresh bread crumbs

1 tsp chopped fresh rosemary

1 Tbsp chopped fresh herbs (mint, parsley, and thyme)

Caper Sauce (page 238)

Preheat the oven to 400°F/200°C. Season the lamb all over with salt and pepper. Heat the butter and oil in a large frying pan over a medium heat and brown the lamb on all sides. Now stand the ribs in a roasting tin opposite each other with the bones interlocked and paint with the mustard.

Mix the bread crumbs and all the herbs together and press down firmly onto the mustard. Cook for about 14 minutes for rare or for longer if you prefer it more well done. Allow to rest for at least 5 minutes, then carve and serve with Caper Sauce (page 238).

Roast Fillet of Lamb

Serves 4

1 lb/455 g best end of lamb fillet or lamb neck slice

1 garlic clove, crushed

2 rosemary leaves, finely chopped

2 Tbsp finely chopped fresh thyme

1 Tbsp finely chopped fresh mint

Salt and freshly ground black pepper

7 oz/200 ml Merlot or Cabernet Sauvignon

1 Tbsp olive oil

A knob of butter

Rub the lamb all over with the garlic, chopped herbs, salt, and pepper. Mix the oil and wine together and pour over the lamb. Place the lamb in the refrigerator and leave to marinate for up to 4 hours, turning over occasionally.

Preheat the oven to 400°F/200°C. Now heat the butter and a splash of olive oil in a hot frying pan until almost smoking and sear the fillet quickly on all sides for just a couple of minutes. Put the fillet in a roasting dish and cover loosely with foil. Roast for 8 to 10 minutes. If you prefer your lamb to be more well done, then cook it for a further 5 minutes. However, be careful not to overcook this, as it tastes wonderful while moist and still pink in the centre. Allow to rest for 5 minutes or so, then slice. Serve with Potato and Celeriac Mash (page 217), asparagus, and homemade Mint Sauce (page 247), with a red wine to match the marinade.

It's a Knockout

"Here," said O'Reilly, walking over from the sideboard to where I sat in an arm chair in the upstairs lounge on a September evening in 1964. He handed me a small sherry and said, "Well done." He helped himself to half a Scotch egg from a plate Kinky had brought up earlier.

I smiled and said, "Thank you." I confess I was feeling a little smug. Not an hour ago, under his supervision of course, I had successfully conducted my first home delivery since my days as a medical student at Belfast's Royal Maternity Hospital.

He sat in another chair, raised his Jameson, said, "Cheers," and took a swig. "I thought that went pretty smoothly," he said. "Mind you, I'm not so sure the home's the place for confinements anymore."

"But," I said, "we were taught that it was all right with the proper selection criteria to ensure that the patient fell into a low-risk category and now we have the flying squad . . ."

He chuckled and said, "What the locals refer to as 'the firing squad.' An ambulance with a senior obstetrical trainee, a midwife, and a couple of bottles of blood? They can render local first aid and get the patient to the hospital for more advanced treatment. I suppose it's nice to have a backup. They certainly saved my bacon a couple of years back."

"Saved your bacon," I said, "Nice figure of speech . . ."

He frowned at me.

I should not have interrupted. "Do go on." I said. "I'm all ears." Certain Hindu devotees reputedly threw themselves under the wheels of a massive temple car, a Juggernaut, and were crushed to death. When O'Reilly was in a mood to reminisce, in like fashion it was easier for me to accept my fate than to try to change the subject.

"It was the year before you came. The schools of medicine and of nursing had each attached one of their students to the practice. Nice youngsters, but one night I could have killed them both."

That was O'Reilly. He had a heart of corn, he was nothing but a teddy bear of a man, but he hid his softness behind a carefully constructed carapace as tough as that of a Galapagos giant tortoise.

"We'd finished for the day; at least we thought we were when the phone rang. I answered. A voice said, 'Doctor O'Reilly, it's the missus. Come quick; she's bleeding.'"

"'Who is this?'

"'Andy McCann.'"

"'I'll be right out.' I knew that his wife, Agnes, was thirty-eight weeks pregnant so I phoned for the flying squad, grabbed my bag, bundled the students into the Rover, and took off. They lived in the housing estate," O'Reilly said. "We got up there in about ten minutes."

I shuddered to think of the trail of unseated cyclists O'Reilly would have left in his wake, but fair play to him, a bleeding pregnant woman was a case where dispatch was definitely indicated. The idea was encapsulated in a nursing adage. "One never ran in a hospital unless," as the nurses said, "there was fire, bleeding— or a good-looking man."

"Andy met us at the door. He said, 'Upstairs.' His eyeballs rolled up into his head, his knees buckled, and he crumpled. The poor devil had fainted right away. 'Right,' says I to the medical student, 'you see to Andy.' You know how narrow the staircases are in those wee estate houses."

"I do." They'd have done service in a mediaeval castle tower where the object of the exercise was to impede an enemy's progress.

"Anyway I went first and the wee nurse followed. We got to the top and I could see Agnes in a double bed in a poky wee room to the right of the landing. 'Follow me,' says I to the nurse and she did. Now," he said, "I'm no sylph . . ."

Which was understating the case. He stood six foot two and must have been a good sixteen stone or, if you prefer, two hundred and twenty four pounds.

"But I just managed to squeeze between the bed and the wall. The nurse had less trouble following me, but to be charitable, the odds of her ever dancing the Sugar Plum Fairy were pretty remote."

I had a mental image of a conversation between a pot and a kettle when the kettle's degree of darkness is being alluded to.

"I called Agnes's name but she was unconscious. Her pulse was thready and racing. The woman was in shock. I threw back the bedclothes and she was lying in a pool of blood. The nurse, who had no obstetric training, said, 'Dear Mother of . . .' and as she swooned she fell on top of me, pinning me between the bed and the wall."

"What did you do?"

"Physically? Nothing, I couldn't get enough purchase to get her off me so I yelled to the student, 'Get up here. Now.'"

"I heard, 'Coming,' a ferocious thump, a gasp, and another body falling." O'Reilly drank and ate more egg. "He never did appear, but about three minutes later the flying squad arrived just as the nurse was coming to. The young obstetrician told me that it looked as if the medical student had been bending over the husband, straightened up suddenly, hit his head on a hanging china cabinet, and . . ."

No further elaboration was required. Despite the potential seriousness of the patient's condition I had trouble not smiling at the thought of the bodies strewn all over the little house.

O'Reilly said, "It was a bloody good thing the ambulance arrived when it did. I could have had three corpses on my hands. Agnes, we later discovered, had a low-lying placenta . . ."

"Always potentially lethal."

"The squad got a couple of pints of blood into her in her bed and in the ambulance. She had a Caesarian section in the hospital, made a fine recovery, and her wee lad is doing very well."

"I'm glad to hear it."

"But I really did think there were going to be two more fatalities."

"I know," I said. "When you started telling me this story you said about the two students, and I quote, 'Nice youngsters but one night I could have killed them both.'"

"I did say that, didn't I?" said O'Reilly, "But it's like 'saved my bacon.'" He fixed me with his gaze. "A what did you call it? I remember. 'Figure of speech.'" He laughed. "Come on," he said. "A bird can't fly on one wing. Let me get you another sherry."

Pork

Dublin Coddle

This is a traditional Irish dish and was often made on a Thursday evening to use up all the leftover meat products in the days when Catholics were not allowed to eat meat on Fridays. Doctor O'Reilly remembers seeing and indeed smelling it being cooked when he worked for Doctor Corrigan in Dublin in the 1930s and he tells me that the great Irish writer James Joyce made several references to it in his books. This is a very simple one-pot meal and can be cooked on top of the stove or in the oven. Just make sure that the pot has a tight-fitting lid.

Serves 4

17½ oz/500 g pork sausages, cut into ½-in/12-mm pieces

8 oz/227 g bacon, roughly chopped

2 oz/56 g butter

2 onions, peeled and sliced

8 potatoes, peeled and thinly sliced

Salt and freshly ground black pepper

10 oz/295 ml chicken stock

A good handful of chopped fresh parsley

If you plan to cook it in the oven then you need to preheat it to 350°F/180°C. Put the sausage, bacon, and most of the butter in a pan over a medium heat and cook for 5 to 10 minutes or until coloured. Spread half of the sliced onions on the bottom of a 1.5L casserole dish and top with half of the potatoes. Next add half of the bacon and sausage mixture and season well with salt and pepper. Repeat the layering process again and pour the stock in last. Add half of the parsley and dot the top with the remaining butter. Cover with a tight-fitting lid and cook for about an hour. Finish with the remaining parsley and serve with some nice bread. My Guinness Bread (page 91) is particularly good with this.

Pork in Mustard Sauce

Serves 4

4 slices pork loin or boneless pork chops, trimmed

1 Tbsp butter, plus extra for greasing

1½ lb/680 g apples, peeled, cored, and thinly sliced

Salt

2 oz/60 ml dry white wine

5 Tbsp/75 ml Dijon mustard

8 oz/235 ml heavy cream

Freshly ground black pepper

Preheat the oven to 400°F/ 200°C. Pound the pork slices or chops between two pieces of parchment with a rolling pin or the base of a heavy saucepan, until they are quite thin.

Butter a casserole dish big enough to spread the pork slices side by side. Cover the base with the apples and bake for 15 minutes.

While the apples are baking, season the pork slices with salt, place with the remaining butter in a frying pan over a medium heat, and cook until they are nicely browned on each side. This should take about 15 minutes.

Now remove the apples from the oven and place the pork on top of the apples in the casserole dish. Place the pan back on the heat, add the wine, and deglaze the pan until the wine has reduced by half. Pour this over the pork. Mix the mustard into the cream, tasting as you go, add some salt and pepper, and pour the mixture over the pork. Return the dish to the oven and bake for a further 25 minutes or so. This is delicious served with Champ (page 209) and just about any other vegetable that you like.

Roast Loin of Pork

Serves 4 to 6

8½ oz/250 ml Guinness

3 oz/90 ml runny honey

7 oz/200 g brown sugar

4½ lb/2 kg boneless pork loin

4 oz/113 ml white wine

A knob of butter

Preheat the oven to 400°F/200°C. Make the glaze by simmering the Guinness, honey, and sugar together in a saucepan until the sugar is dissolved and the liquid is reduced by half.

Put the pork in a roasting dish and cook for 20 minutes. Reduce the oven temperature to 350°F/180°C. Remove the pork from the oven and baste all over with the glaze. Return the pork to the oven and cook, basting occasionally with the glaze. Cook for a further hour or so until the meat is tender and cooked through. Remove from the oven and place on a carving board. While the pork is resting, add any remaining glaze to the roasting tin together with the wine and deglaze the pan on a stovetop over a high heat. Whisk the butter into the simmering liquid and allow to thicken into a delicious gravy.

Slice the pork into thick slices and place in a serving dish with the gravy drizzled on top. Serve Roast Potatoes (page 219) that you have cooked alongside the Pork and Colcannon (page 210).

Stuffed Pork Tenderloin

Serves 4

1 oz/28 g butter, plus extra for buttering the parchment

1 onion, finely chopped

3 oz/85 g mushrooms, finely chopped

2 Tbsp chopped fresh parsley

½ tsp dried thyme

4 oz/113 g fresh bread crumbs

Salt and freshly ground black pepper

1 (1-lb/455-g) pork tenderloin

4 or 5 slices bacon

Preheat the oven to 350°F/180°C. Melt the butter in a pan, then fry the onion gently for a few minutes until it is translucent and soft but not coloured. Add the mushrooms and then the parsley and thyme. Cook for a few minutes, add the bread crumbs, and season with salt and pepper.

Split the tenderloin lengthwise (butterflied). Then, using a rolling pin or a meat mallet, batter it on both halves to flatten it. Spread the stuffing on one side of the tenderloin and place the other half on top. Wrap the strips of bacon around the pork, place it on a piece of buttered parchment or foil, and close it loosely by scrunching the top and sides. Bake in the top rack of the preheated oven for about 1 hour. Then open the parchment or foil and cook about 10 minutes longer. Allow to rest for 10 minutes or so, then slice and serve.

NOTE:

This is very good served with applesauce or apple fritters.

Toad in the Hole

The country folk claim that this dish came by its name because it resembled a toad or maybe a frog peeping out of a hole when it had awakened from hibernation. Then when it climbed out of the mud, leaving an imprint of its shape behind, it was just like removing a sausage from the batter in which it had been cooked. Ma says they did not actually eat toads, which are probably quite poisonous, but they used any bits and pieces of leftover meat or sausages baked in the batter, which helped to make a meager amount of food feed more mouths.

> *Serves 2*
> 2 eggs
> 4 oz/113 g self-rising flour
> A pinch of baking powder
> A splash of milk
> A few thyme leaves
> Salt and freshly ground black pepper
> 4 oz/113 g pork cocktail sausages, cooked

Preheat the oven to 425°F/225°C. Beat the eggs in a bowl. Continue to whisk and add the flour and baking powder gradually, together with enough milk to make a thickish batter the consistency of cream. Add the thyme leaves, season with salt and pepper, and pour the batter into a greased 7-inch casserole dish. Place the sausages on top. Bake for 10 to 12 minutes, until the batter is well risen and golden brown. Serve.

Fish

Fish Pie

Serves 4

FILLING

20 oz/590 ml milk
1 or 2 bay leaves
Salt and freshly ground black pepper
1 lb/455 g mixed fish such as salmon, cod, snapper, or haddock
4 oz/113 g shrimp or prawns, peeled
4 oz/113 g scallops
2 oz/56 g butter
2 Tbsp all-purpose flour
2 Tbsp chopped fresh parsley

TOPPING

2 lb/910 g floury potatoes, peeled and quartered
5 oz/150 ml light cream
1 oz/28 g butter
2 Tbsp grated cheddar cheese or Parmesan cheese
Salt and freshly ground black pepper

Preheat the oven to 400°F/200°C. Grease a 10 by 8-inch/25 by 20-cm pie dish.

FOR THE FILLING:
Bring the milk and and bay leaves to the boil in a large saucepan and season with salt and pepper. Add the uncooked fish and shellfish, omitting the shrimp if it has been precooked. Simmer very gently for about 3 minutes. Cover and leave while you prepare the topping.

FOR THE TOPPING:

Boil the potatoes until soft, drain, and mash well with the cream and butter. Season with salt and pepper to taste.

Meanwhile, drain the fish, reserving the milk, and discard the bay leaf. Remove any skin or bones from the fish, break into bite-size pieces, and spread it in the pie dish with the cooked shrimp. Melt the butter in a saucepan and carefully stir in the flour. Cook gently for a couple of minutes without letting the roux (a fancy French word for the flour and butter mixture) brown. Now add the milk to the roux very gradually with the parsley and season with salt and pepper. Bring to the boil and simmer gently for 3 or 4 minutes, stirring all the time. Then pour the sauce over the fish.

It's time now to cover with the potato topping. Just spread it across the top of the fish and sauce mixture, pressing down lightly with a fork and covering it from edge to edge. Dot it all over with butter or a little cheese. Bake for about 30 minutes, or until nicely browned. Serve.

Kinky's Note:

This is also delicious when topped with Champ (page 209) which has been dotted with grated cheese or butter.

Kedgeree

This is very good with either my Irish Wheaten Bread (page 94) or Guinness Bread (page 91). Doctor O'Reilly likes it for breakfast nearly as much as he likes my kippers but it is also a very appetising lunch dish. Himself is very fond of it and he told me that this was one of those dishes that came from India in Victorian times and had originated as a means of using up leftovers from the previous evening at breakfast time before there were refrigerators.

Serves 6 to 8

1½ lb/680 g undyed smoked haddock (or use half salmon and half haddock)

19 oz/560 ml water

2 bay leaves

1½ oz/42 g butter

1 onion, finely chopped

8 oz/227 g long-grain basmati rice

1 heaped Tbsp medium curry powder

3 Tbsp heavy cream

3 Tbsp chopped fresh parsley

2 Tbsp chopped scallion

Juice of ½ a lemon, plus lemon wedges for serving

Freshly ground black pepper

3 large hard-boiled eggs, quartered

Bring the fish, water, and bay leaves to the boil in a large saucepan and simmer gently for about 10 minutes. Drain the fish, reserving the cooking liquid as you will use this to cook the rice, and discard the bay leaves. Now flake the fish into bite-size chunks and make sure that no bones remain.

Melt the butter in a large frying pan and fry the onion gently, but don't let it colour. Add the rice, curry powder, and reserved liquid and cook for the time recommended on the packet, adding more water if necessary.

When the rice is cooked, add the cream, parsley, scallion, lemon juice, pepper, and finally the flaked fish. Stir gently and place the hard-boiled eggs on top. You can keep this warm in a very low oven, covered with a lid, for about 20 minutes. I like to put it in a silver chafing dish and leave it on the sideboard so that everyone can help themselves at breakfast time.

Mustard Baked Fish

Here's another simple fish dish that's very quick and makes a tasty but light lunch.

Serves 4
4 6 oz/170 g fillets of white fish such as cod, haddock, or red snapper
1 tsp salt
Freshly ground black pepper
8 oz/235 ml whipping cream or crème fraîche
3 shallots, finely chopped
2 Tbsp Dijon mustard
1 Tbsp whole-grain mustard
1 Tbsp water
2 tsp capers, drained
Chopped fresh parsley

Preheat the oven to 425°F/200°C. Grease a baking dish of a size that can hold the fillets in a single layer. Season the fish on both sides and lay skin-side down (if the fillets are skin-on), in the dish.

Combine the cream, shallots, mustards, water, and capers in a bowl, season with salt and pepper, and pour over the fish, making sure to cover all the fillets. Cover and bake for about 15 minutes, then sprinkle with parsley and serve with garden peas and crusty bread.

Potted Herrings

This is a very tasty and easy dish that Ma used to make in the summertime when the herrings were in season. We had a travelling fish seller who came every week in his horse and cart, and his cry of "Ardglass herrings, Ardglass herrings!" brought the delighted housewives onto the street to buy his fish. Ardglass was, and still is, a famous fishing port on the Irish Sea near to the mouth of Strangford Lough where himself likes to go wildfowling.

It was handy to have these herrings ready in the refrigerator when the Doctor was on call and I could never be quite sure when he would return from his home visits.

These will keep for several days in a refrigerator and taste even better after leaving overnight.

Herrings are members of the sardine family and have lots of little bones. Somehow they just seem to melt when cooked like this.

Serves 4

8 herrings, cleaned, scaled, and wiped dry inside and out with heads and tails
   removed

4 bay leaves

1 onion, chopped

1 tsp pickling spice

Freshly ground black pepper

Equal parts water and malt vinegar

Preheat the oven to 325°F/160°C. Roll the herrings from the tail end and place side by side in a 8 by 6-inch (20 by 15-cm) baking dish so that each one supports the other and prevents it from unrolling. Cover with the onion, bay leaves, pickling spice, pepper to taste, vinegar, and water. Cover the dish with a lid or with aluminium foil and cook for about 35 minutes. Allow to cool before serving with buttered Irish Wheaten Bread (page 94) or baby new potatoes cooked in their skins and slathered in butter.

Salmon in a Pickle

Serves 4 to 6

36 oz/1 kg skinless salmon fillet cut into 6 pieces

8 oz/235 ml distilled malt vinegar

8 oz/235 ml water

4 oz/113 g sugar

4 Tbsp tomato ketchup or chili sauce

1 tsp salt

4 onions, finely chopped

2 Tbsp pickling spice

Preheat the oven to 400°F/200°C. Butter an 8 by 6-inch (20 by 15-cm) dish, place the salmon fillets in the dish, and set aside.

Combine the vinegar, water, sugar, ketchup, and salt in a large saucepan and bring to the boil. Stir in the onions and pickling spice and pour over the salmon. Cover with foil and cook for 10 to 12 minutes, until cooked through. Allow to cool and place in the refrigerator overnight.

Remove from the poaching liquid and serve with a green salad.

Simple Baked Fish

Ma was very fond of this dish and of course it always seemed different depending on the fish used. And what a variety of fish the local fishermen brought in. She did, however, use strong country cheddar cheese instead of Parmesan.

Serves 4

1 Tbsp butter, plus extra for the dish

3 potatoes, peeled and sliced

2 onions, sliced

2 garlic cloves, crushed

Salt and freshly ground black pepper

1½ lb/680 g white fish, such as cod, sea bass, or turbot

1 Tbsp chopped fresh thyme

3 tomatoes, peeled and sliced

A pinch of saffron

2 oz/60 ml fresh orange juice

3 Tbsp dry white wine

2 oz/56 g Parmesan cheese, grated

4 oz/113 g fresh bread crumbs

Preheat the oven to 375°F/190°C. Butter the sides and base of a medium casserole dish. Blanch the potatoes for 2 or 3 minutes in boiling water and drain. Sauté the onions in the butter for a few minues over a medium heat, add the garlic and cook until soft.

Layer half of the potatoes in the casserole and cover with half of the onion mixture. Season with salt and pepper. Lay the fish on top and sprinkle with thyme leaves and place the tomato slices over this. Finish with the remaining onions and top with the remaining potatoes; season again with salt and pepper. Crumble the saffron into the orange juice, then pour the orange juice and wine over the casserole and finally sprinkle the cheese and bread crumbs on top.

Bake for 30 to 45 minutes, until the potatoes and fish are cooked and most of the liquid has been absorbed. I like to serve this with fresh crusty bread to mop up the extra juices.

Kinky's Note:

To skin tomatoes easily, take a sharp knife and make a cut through the skin round the circumference of the tomato. Place in a bowl of boiling water for 1 minute. Transfer to a bowl of icy cold water and the skin will peel off very easily.

Forms,
Forms,
Forms

Doctor Fingal O'Reilly was a courteous man, always willing to make allowances, until somebody really got his goat. Then he became a patient man who subscribed to the adage attributed to Talleyrand, "Revenge is a dish best eaten cold." I can still see him in action as he was when I first joined the practice in 1964.

"I think we're in luck, Barry," O'Reilly said. "With all the snow . . ." He pointed out the window of the upstairs lounge to where the roof of the Presbyterian church opposite was a foot deep in the sparkling white stuff and one side of the steeple looked as if it had been sheathed in cotton wool, "I don't think we'll be having the promised visit from that woman from the ministry." He rubbed his hands in delight and reached for another slice of hot buttered barmback. His third.

O'Reilly, I had learned, while being the soul of sweetness and light to widows, small children, and stray cats—he had after all taken in Lady Macbeth, who'd been left in a basket on his doorstep—had a deep abiding hatred for bureaucracy and form filling. I had learned it at firsthand last week when "that woman" had made her first appearance at Number One Main Street. I'd had the luck, or perhaps misfortune is a better word, to be present.

Kinky had stuck her head round the surgery door. Morning surgery had run late, was just over, and O'Reilly was hungry. "Excuse me, sir, but there does be a Miss Pilkington here. She says she's come down from Stormont Castle in Belfast from the Ministry of Health, so. I have explained that it is your lunchtime but she does be most insistent she speak with you at once." Kinky's usually animated features remained firmly at rest. Her lips were compressed into a thin line.

"Oh Lord." O'Reilly rolled his eyes to heaven. "I'd forgotten about her. She phoned last week. It's to do with some blasted forms I've not filled in right." He glanced at the window and for a moment I thought he was going to do a runner. He sighed, then said, "Show her in."

Kinky opened the door wide and was jostled aside by a tall, angular, middle-aged woman.

O'Reilly rose from his swivel chair. I slipped from where I'd been sitting on the examining couch. Men stood when a lady entered.

Her stride was purposeful as her sensible low-heeled brogues carried her across the carpet. "O'Reilly?" she said in a harsh tenor. I noted she did not use his title.

She carried an attaché case. Her grey double-breasted raincoat had padded shoulders. I thought of how my mother had dressed in the late forties. She wore a tam-o'-shanter perched to one side of severely cropped iron-grey hair. She peered at O'Reilly with pale eyes from behind wire-rimmed spectacles perched on the bridge

TOP LEFT
Scotch Eggs

TOP RIGHT
Smoked Salmon with Cream Cheese

LEFT
*Mussels in Guinness with Potato
and Pumpkin Seed Bread*

BELOW
*Steak and Mushroom Pie with Spicy Red Cabbage
and Champ Topping*

RIGHT
Roast Rack of Lamb and Caper Sauce

TOP LEFT
Kedgeree

TOP RIGHT
Eton Mess with Ginger Biscuits

LEFT
Guinness Gingerbread with Ice Cream

RIGHT
Tomato Soup; Jerusalem Artichoke Soup,
Croutons, and Maple Syrup; Pea and Mint Soup

TOP
Dorothy Tinman, Rhythms of
the Tide, *2012. Oil on canvas.*

BOTTOM LEFT
Dorothy Tinman, Crested
Wave, *2014. Oil on canvas.*

BOTTOM RIGHT
Dorothy Tinman, The Sea,
The Sea, *2015. Oil on canvas.*

of an aquiline nose. She wore no makeup. Thin lips drooped at eight twenty.

"That's me," he said in a small voice. His smile was forced.

She thrust out her right hand, forcing him to do her the courtesy of shaking it—this, please remember, in a class-ridden society in which handshakes were only ever offered by a superior to a lesser mortal. Try to imagine Her Majesty being offered a hand by a coal miner. It doesn't ring true, does it? "I am Miss Hermione Pilkington, B.A., principal officer in the Ministry of Health."

No courtesy title for Doctor O'Reilly but she wanted her full dress formalities.

"Yes," said O'Reilly. "And that's Doctor Laverty."

She ignored me.

"Will you have a seat?" O'Reilly asked.

"I prefer to stand."

This meant, of course, that neither O'Reilly nor I could sit.

She opened her briefcase, took out a file, and thrust it at O'Reilly. "Open it."

Apparently, "please" was not in her vocabulary.

O'Reilly did. I noticed that a certain paleness in the tip of his boxer's bent nose, a sure sign that, if not yet coming to the boil, my senior colleague was beginning to simmer.

"These are the last series of Ministry Claim Form B-two-oh-six-slash-forty-one-A submitted by you, O'Reilly for the last two weeks . . ."

Two weeks of a murderous flu epidemic during which time O'Reilly and I had barely enough time to eat and sleep, never mind fill in some pettifogging pieces of paperwork.

She shook her head and for a moment I thought she was going to stamp her foot. "Every one of them, every single one, is incorrect." She waved an admonitory finger. "How on earth do you expect us to keep our statistics up to date without the proper forms being filled in?"

"I can see that it might be difficult." O'Reilly's tone was placatory. His nose tip alabaster. I was quite sure that had Principal Officer Miss Hermione Pilkington B.A. been a man he'd now be on the receiving end of a tongue lashing if not a straight left, but O'Reilly was of the old school.

She stepped up to him, took one form, laid it on his desk, and said, "Pen."

O'Reilly produced one and for the next five minutes (at least it seemed like five minutes), she instructed him in the minutiae of dealing with Form B-two-oh-six-slash-forty-one-A as a school mistress might instruct a dim five-year-old in his ABCs.

"I," she said with the stress that President Charles de Gaulle reserved for his emphatic *Moi*, "am leaving the folder here. You will complete the forms correctly. I will return in one week to ensure that you have completed the task and any others that have accrued during the intervening period. Is that understood?"

"Yes," said O'Reilly.

"Good." She spun on her heel and, without as much as a by-your-leave, strode out.

I heard the front door slam.

O'Reilly shook his head. "I," he said, "hate paper work, and detest that species *Homo administratus*. It's a good thing that particular one didn't live in Salem, Massachusetts, in sixteen ninety two. She's a witch." He managed a grin. "Still, worse things happen at sea. Come on, let's get lunch. Kinky's making pea and ham soup and buttermilk pancakes."

And in the hurly-burly of the practice of the next week I'd forgotten about Miss Pilkington until the moment he'd said that the snow would prevent a visit from "that woman."

Of course he was wrong.

Kinky came into the lounge. "I am sorry sir, but the lady from the ministry's here."

"What? She can't be."

"She can, bye, and I have put her in the surgery."

"Bloody hell," said O'Reilly. "Come on then, Barry." He rose and I followed.

She was waiting, arms folded, lips pursed.

"Gracious, Miss Pilkington," said O'Reilly. "Those forms must be important for you to risk coming here in this weather."

"They are," she said, "and I was fortunate. An army helicopter had come with a VIP officer from the barracks here to Stormont Castle. They kindly gave me a ride on their way home."

"Decent of them," said O'Reilly and took a long pause before adding, "I should have thought it would be bloody cold riding a broom in this weather."

SIDE DISHES

Chutney

You can make chutney with virtually any fruit or vegetable that you have in abundance. If you are making chutney for long-term storage you must sterilize the canning jars. If you are planning to make a lot of jelly, jam, and chutney then it would be a good investment to buy a preserving pan sometimes called a jam pan. These are usually made of heavy-gauge aluminum and are large enough and heavy based so that you can bring the jam or chutney to a high temperature and, in the case of chutney making, to enable the vinegar to reduce and the chutney to thicken.

Smaller amounts of chutney for immediate use do not need to be stored in canning jars and may be kept in the fridge in plastic containers, or may be frozen. However, some chutney does improve with keeping and where that is the case I have indicated. These chutneys will need to be bottled in sterilised jars and stored in a cool, dark cupboard. It is not necessary to refrigerate them.

Apple Chutney

This simple apple version is quick, easy, and delicious with cold leftover lamb, ham, or pork and very good with a cheese board.

Makes 6 to 8 8 oz/227 g jars
2¼ lb/1 kg tart apples, peeled, cored, and chopped
18 oz/535 ml cider vinegar
1 lb/455 g onions, chopped
8 oz/227 g brown sugar
3½ oz/100 g raisins or sultanas
1 (2-in/5-cm) piece fresh ginger, grated
1 red or green chile, seeds reserved
2 garlic cloves, crushed
1 tsp salt

Combine all the ingredients in a large saucepan and bring slowly to a simmer, stirring until the sugar has dissolved. Now cook gently over a low heat for about 1 hour, stirring occasionally. Taste after about 30 minutes and add the seeds from the chile if you would like a hotter chutney. Continue cooking for a further 30 minutes, stirring more frequently as the mixture thickens. When the chutney has cooled down, place in sterilised jars and cover with lids. Store in a cool, dark place. If you can wait, this chutney will taste better in about a month's time.

Beet Chutney

Makes 2 8 oz/227 g jars

1 Tbsp olive oil

1 red onion, finely chopped

1 garlic clove, crushed

1 (1-in/2.5-cm) piece fresh ginger, grated

1 tsp mustard seeds

12 oz/340 g beets, cooked and chopped

½ apple (Pink Lady is nice), peeled, cored, and finely shredded

2½ oz/75 ml cider vinegar

2 oz/56 g sugar

Salt and freshly ground black pepper

Heat the oil in a large pan over a medium heat, add the onion, garlic, and ginger and cook until soft. Add the mustard seeds and cook until they pop. Add the beets, apple, vinegar, and sugar and cook for a few minutes until the chutney has thickened. Season with salt and pepper to taste and allow to cool before serving. Transfer to jars or a plastic lidded container such as Tupperware. This chutney may be kept, covered, for two or three weeks in the refrigerator. If you have more than you need for immediate use it can be stored in the freezer in freezer-proof containers.

Cranberry Chutney

Makes 2 8 oz/227 g jars

1 lb/455 g cranberries

8 oz/227 g brown sugar

4 oz/113 g raisins

4 oz/120 ml water

2½ oz/75 ml cider vinegar

1 (1-in/2.5-cm) piece fresh ginger, grated

2 tsp ground cinnamon

½ tsp ground cloves

1 onion, finely chopped

1 tart apple, peeled, cored, and finely chopped

Combine the cranberries, sugar, raisins, water, vinegar, ginger, cinnamon, and cloves in a large saucepan. Bring to a boil, then simmer over low heat until the cranberries start to pop, about 5 minutes. Add the onion and apple and continue to cook, stirring occasionally, until the mixture begins to thicken, 5 to 10 more minutes. Transfer to two 8-ounce/227-g jars and allow to cool slightly. Cover and refrigerate overnight before using. If you will not be able to use within about three weeks just freeze the surplus in a freezer-proof container.

Mint Chutney

Makes 1 serving

A large handful of young mint leaves

1 large apple (such as Granny Smith or Pink Lady), peeled and cored.

2 oz/56 g chopped red onion

Juice of ½ lemon or lime

A pinch of sugar

A pinch of salt

A pinch of cayenne pepper

Process all the ingredients in a blender until coarsely chopped. Season and store in an airtight container. This will keep for about five days in the fridge.

Plum Chutney

This chutney is particularly good with pork or ham dishes.

Makes 2 8 oz/227 g jars
1 lb/455 g red or yellow plums, pitted
6 oz/170 g sugar
3½ oz/105 ml cider or apple vinegar
1 (1-in/2.5-cm) piece fresh ginger, grated
1 garlic clove, crushed
1 tsp ground ginger
1 tsp ground cinnamon

Combine all the ingredients in a saucepan and bring to the boil, stirring until the sugar has dissolved. Continue to simmer gently for 20 to 30 minutes, until the chutney has thickened and the plums are tender. Transfer to sterilised jars. Allow to cool before using. This chutney will keep for up to three months in a cool, dark cupboard or may be frozen in freezer-proof containers.

Vegetable
Side Dishes

Champ

Champ is very popular in Ireland as an accompaniment for other dishes. In fact I do believe it was invented by the Irish. It was cheap and nutritious and it might have been eaten as often as three times a week. I loved it when Ma would sometimes beat a raw egg into it just before serving but this had to be done very quickly because the champ cooled with the addition of the cold egg.

In Ireland we have a somewhat unkind expression, "Someone is as thick as champ," meaning that he's not very intelligent.

This makes a nice change from just having mashed potatoes as a topping on savoury dishes. It looks good too when dotted with butter or cheese and browned under a hot grill or broiler. If you have any left over, which is extremely unlikely, you can use it to make Irish Potato Bread (page 93).

Serves 4 to 6
2 lb/910 g potatoes, peeled and quartered
1 bunch scallions, chopped
8 oz/235 ml milk
Salt and freshly ground black pepper
2 oz/56 g butter

Boil the potatoes until soft, drain, and mash well. In a separate pan, cook the scallions with the milk and seasoning at a slow simmer until soft. This only takes a few minutes, but keep watching it to make sure that it does not boil over. Now add this together with the butter to the mashed potatoes and mix well. Serve.

Colcannon

From the Irish *cál ceannann* meaning "white-headed cabbage." In some parts of Scotland it is called rumbledethumps.

Serves 4 to 6
1¾ lb/800 g floury potatoes, peeled and quartered
4 oz/113 g curly kale or spring cabbage
1 bunch scallions
4 oz/113 g butter
2 slices bacon, cooked and chopped (optional)
Salt and freshly ground black pepper
Chopped fresh parsley and chives

Boil the potatoes for about 15 minutes until just soft. Drain them and dry over the residual heat on the stovetop. Blanch the kale for 1 minute. Drain, then dry in a clean tea towel or on paper towels and roughly chop with the scallion (or pulse the kale and scallions in a blender for about 10 seconds).

Mash the potatoes with a potato masher (not the food processor) and add most of the butter. Stir in the kale, scallions, and bacon (if using) and season with salt and pepper to taste. Make a well in the centre and drop in the remaining butter. Sprinkle chopped parsley and chives on top and serve.

Crispy Flourless Potato Cake

This works very well with an Ulster Fry (page 111) instead of Irish Potato Bread (page 93), or as an accompaniment to many savory dishes.

Serves 4
1 lb/455 g russet potatoes, unpeeled
½ onion, grated
Salt
1 oz/28 g butter

Boil the potatoes and allow to cool, then peel and coarsely grate them. Combine with the onion and season with salt. Heat half the butter in a nonstick frying pan over a medium heat, pile in the potato and onion mixture, and flatten this down. Cook for about 10 minutes until you see the edges starting to brown. Now slide the potato cake onto a plate, then place the pan upside down over the plate and transfer the cake, cooked-side up, into the pan. You may want to add the rest of the butter round the edges now. Cook for another 10 minutes until the underside is crisp. Cut into wedges and serve hot.

Bacon and Leek Pudding

This is a nice accompaniment for a roast beef dish or a simple weekday sausage meal.

Serves 4

1 lb 2 oz/500 g leeks

4 oz/113 g bacon, chopped

3 oz/85 g butter

1 Tbsp fresh thyme leaves

2 Tbsp dry white wine

7 oz/210 ml heavy cream

Salt and freshly ground black pepper

4 oz/113 g brioche, broken into ½-in/12-mm chunks

3 oz/85 g Parmesan cheese, grated

Preheat the oven to 400°F/200°C. Grease a 8 by 6-inch/20 cm by 15-cm baking dish.

Slice the leeks and wash very carefully in several changes of salted water. Fry the bacon until crisp and set aside. Heat half of the butter in the frying pan and gently cook the leeks and thyme until soft. Add the wine and cook until reduced by half. Add the cream, season with salt and pepper, and reduce again. Pour into the baking dish and mix in the chopped bacon.

Melt the rest of the butter in another frying pan, add the brioche chunks, and fry until golden. Sprinkle the bread over the top of the casserole, top with the cheese, and bake for 20 to 30 minutes. Serve.

Himmel und Urde

This is a traditional German dish often served with pork. It was also popular in Ireland, as the two main ingredients were so often grown together and the free-roaming pigs in the farm yard would snaffle about in the orchards eating the windfalls. The meaning of the name is quite lovely too: Heaven and Earth. The Irish probably just called it mashed potatoes with apple. I like to use almost equal quantities of potato and Bramley apples but you can adjust this as you like.

Serves 4 to 6
2 lb/910 g potatoes, peeled and quartered
1½ lb/680 g tart apples, peeled, cored, and cut into chunks
2 oz/56 g butter
A good splash of whipping cream
Salt and freshly ground black pepper

Place the potatoes and apples in a large saucepan, cover with water, bring to the boil, and cook until just soft. Drain off the water and place over a low heat to dry. Add most of the butter and the cream and mash all together. Season with salt and pepper to taste, then place in a serving dish and dot with the remaining butter. Keep warm in the oven 'til ready to serve.

Kinky's Note:
For a change, mix crispy chopped bacon through the mash.

Marinated Mushrooms

Serves 4 to 6

5 oz/150 ml white wine vinegar

3 Tbsp extra-virgin olive oil

Juice of ½ lemon

1 small onion or 2 shallots, finely chopped

1 garlic clove, crushed

1 bay leaf

Salt and freshly ground black pepper

1 lb/455 g white mushrooms or cremini mushrooms, trimmed and quartered

Chopped fresh cilantro

Combine the vinegar, olive oil, lemon juice, onion, garlic, and bay leaf in a saucepan. Bring to the boil and simmer for just a few minutes until the onion is cooked. Season with salt and pepper to taste and pour over the mushrooms. Cover and refrigerate overnight. Remove the bay leaf, garnish with chopped cilantro, and serve. These keep, refrigerated, for about a week in a sealed container.

Lemon Rice

Serves 4

A knob of butter

1 small onion, chopped, or 2 shallots, chopped

8 oz/227 g long grain rice

Grated zest and juice of 1 lemon

16 oz/475 ml chicken stock

Salt and freshly ground black pepper

½ tsp chopped fresh tarragon

Melt the butter in a medium saucepan and gently fry the onion for a few minutes without browning. Add the rice and lemon zest and juice and stir once. Add the chicken stock and season with salt and pepper. Cover and simmer for about 15 minutes, by which time the stock should be absorbed. Stir the tarragon through the rice.

Onion Pudding

Serves 4
1 oz/28 g butter
1 lb 2 oz/500 g mild sweet onions, finely sliced
2 eggs
5 oz/150 ml milk
1 oz/28 g all-purpose flour
Salt and freshly ground black pepper

Preheat the oven to 450°F/230°C. Melt the butter in a lidded frying pan, add the onions, cover, and cook gently for about half an hour without letting them colour. Whisk together the eggs, milk, and flour until smooth and season with salt and pepper. Stir in the onions and pour into a well-buttered casserole. Cook for 20 to 25 minutes, until well risen and coloured. Serve.

Potato and Celeriac Mash

Serves 4 to 6

1 lb/455 g celeriac, peeled

1 lb/455 g russet potatoes, peeled

2 oz/60 ml heavy cream

2 oz/56 g butter

Salt and freshly ground black pepper

Slice away the rough outside skins of the celeriac and chop into 1-in/2.5-cm chunks. Peel and chop the potatoes into slightly larger chunks than the celeriac. (This will ensure that both vegetables cook evenly and are ready at the same time.) Now put them into a pan of boiling salted water to just cover them and cook for 15 to 20 minutes, until tender. Drain, mash and dry off over a low heat. Add the cream and butter, season with salt and pepper to taste, and serve.

Potato Gratin

Serves 4 to 6

2 garlic cloves, peeled

Butter

2¼ lb/910 g waxy potatoes, peeled and thinly sliced

24 oz/710 ml milk

Salt

1 egg

6 oz/170 g cheddar cheese or Gruyère cheese, shredded

Ground nutmeg

Freshly ground black pepper

Preheat the oven to 400°F/200°C. Rub the sides and base of a 9 by 13-inch/23 by 33-cm baking dish with the garlic, then chop the garlic and set aside. Butter the dish well.

Rinse the potatoes well in cold water and drain them. Bring the milk to the boil with a little salt, add the potatoes and the chopped garlic, and simmer very gently for about 5 minutes. Drain the potatoes and reserve the milk.

Beat together the egg, half the cheese, the nutmeg, and salt and pepper in a bowl. While still whisking, add the milk. Layer the potatoes in the casserole dish and pour the milk mixture over. Sprinkle the rest of the cheese on top and dot the surface generously with butter. Cook for 20 minutes, by which time the top should be golden and the potatoes cooked. If they are not soft when tested with a fork, leave to cook for another 5 minutes or so. If the top is becoming too brown, cover with a piece of foil.

VARIATION
Try this with alternating layers of thinly sliced parboiled carrot or parsnip or both.

Roast Potatoes

Serves 6 to 8

5 Tbsp duck or goose fat or canola oil

8 potatoes peeled and cut into halves or thirds if large

1 tbsp sea salt

Preheat the oven to 400°F/200°C. Put the fat or oil into a large 9 by 13-inch/23 by 33-cm roasting pan in the oven. Parboil the potatoes for about 5 minutes. Drain them in a colander and return them to the hot saucepan. Add the sea salt to the potatoes, replace the lid and give them a good shake. This gives the potato edges a rough texture and improves the crunchiness of the finished roast potatoes.

Empty the potatoes into the roasting pan and mix until they are coated with the hot fat. Return the pan to the oven for about 20 minutes. They will now be starting to colour and should be turned over and cooked for another 20 to 30 minutes or until they are golden brown and crunchy. Drain on paper towels.

Spicy Red Cabbage

Serves 8 to 10

4 oz/113 g raisins

3 Tbsp dark brown sugar

1 garlic clove, crushed

1 tsp ground cinnamon

½ tsp ground nutmeg

¼ tsp ground cloves

Salt and freshly ground black pepper

1 (2 lb/910 g) red cabbage, cored and shredded

1 lb/455 g tart apples, peeled, cored, and shredded

2 red onions, sliced

5 oz/150 ml apple cider

2 Tbsp white wine vinegar or cider vinegar

1 bay leaf

Combine the raisins, sugar, garlic, cinnamon, nutmeg, cloves, and salt and pepper to taste. Layer the cabbage, apples, and onion into a Dutch oven, sprinkling the sugar mixture in between the layers as you go. Pour the cider and vinegar over the top and drop in the bay leaf.

This dish may be cooked either in the oven or on the stovetop but I think it is easier to do it on the stovetop because you will need to stir it from time to time.

Cover with a tight-fitting lid and cook slowly for 2 or 3 hours, stirring occasionally. If you like you can leave the lid off for the last 30 minutes to reduce the fluid and concentrate the flavour. Remove the bay leaf and serve.

If cooking in the oven, bake at 350°F /180°C for 2 or 3 hours and remove the lid for the last 30 minutes.

This dish may be prepared well in advance and frozen.

Kinky's Note:

Whilst Bramley apples would have been the cooking apples of choice in Ulster, if they are not available, try using Braeburn or any other slightly tart variety.

Yorkshire Pudding

Yorkshire pudding is traditionally served with roast beef and is a similar batter to that used in the Toad in the Hole recipe. In poorer families, both, indeed, had a similar purpose. With the Toad, the intention was to make a small amount of meat stretch a bit further, while the Yorkshire pudding was often served before the meat course, thus providing a cheap way to take the edge off of the appetite and make the more expensive meat go further. In poorer households, the Yorkshire pudding served with gravy was often the only course. Doctor O'Reilly tells me that it dates back to the eighteenth century and came from the North of England. He likes me to serve it with a lamb roast fillet or roast pork, as well as roast beef.

Makes about 12
4 oz/113 g all-purpose flour
Salt and freshly ground black pepper
2 eggs
10 oz/295 ml milk
4 Tbsp goose fat, lard, or sunflower or canola oil

Preheat the oven to 400°F/200°C. Sift the flour and seasonings into a bowl and whisk in the eggs. Add the milk slowly and whisk until you have a smooth batter. Chill in the refrigerator until ready to use.

Distribute the fat or oil evenly between the cupcake or muffin pans and heat in the oven until it is very hot and almost smoking. Pour the batter into the pans and return to the oven. Bake for 15 to 20 minutes, until well risen and golden brown. (Do not open the door while the puddings are cooking or they might collapse.) Leave for a few more minutes if necessary. Prick with a toothpick to allow the steam to escape. Serve immediately.

Kinky's Note:

This batter can be made up to three days in advance but you should bring it back to room temperature before cooking.

You
Win Some,
You
Lose Some

"Right," said O'Reilly, parking himself in an armchair, "not long to the start." He leant forward and switched on the television that had a small room of its own at Number One Main Street because, as he had once explained, "I don't like the baleful eye watching me in my lounge."

He clutched a glass of Jameson's Irish whiskey. Being on call, I sipped a C & C Club Orange.

The screen flickered, looked like a snowstorm, then produced a distorted black-and-white picture of a man's head and shoulders that shimmied like my sister Kate.

O'Reilly muttered something, rose, and struck the top of the set a single thump.

I swear there was instant resolution of the picture and the commentator, David Coleman, clunky microphone to his lips, looked a bit as if he'd been the recipient of the blow.

O'Reilly growled, "And I'll take no cheek from electrical devices either."

Coleman's plummy English tones came from the set's speakers, "Welcome to Aintree for the running of the one hundred and nineteenth Grand National, the world's toughest steeplechase. The course is four miles, three and a half furlongs. The forty-seven horses will attempt to jump thirty jumps over two circuits of the track. . . ."

O'Reilly leant forward and turned down the volume. "He'll blether on for a while before we get the real action. I'm all set on this one. I've studied the racing form of every horse and I've got the inside word from Fergus Finnegan . . ."

I'd treated the Marquis of Ballybucklebo's jockey for an eye infection last year. He was renowned for his ability to predict the outcome of horse races.

"Fergus says there's a great Irish horse, Crobeg, running at a hundred to one. I've five pounds on him. You know, Barry," he said, "it's a great science putting bets on horses. You really have to bring a trained mind like mine to bear."

"Good luck," I said, recalling with great clarity a horse called Battle Cruiser that O'Reilly had backed at a point-to-point last year. The animal had a reputation for loving to jump fences. Regrettably, it had gone over the first fence it saw—the perimeter fence—and it hadn't come back. I had felt it tactful not to mention that.

"Aye," said O'Reilly, taking a pull on his whiskey, "Did I ever tell you about the time in Dublin . . . hang on, your man Coleman's talking about the tote board. We're going to get the starting prices." He turned up the volume.

". . . the favourite, Freddie is at seven to two . . ."

And I wasn't going to get to hear whatever O'Reilly was going to tell me about.

"Jasus," said O'Reilly, "put down two quid to win seven? Not me."

Coleman said, "The Rip, nine to one. Pat Taafe's up on Quintin Bay and with such a famous jockey the odds are twenty-five to one. . . ."

O'Reilly said, "The bookies use their loafs before they call the odds. I said and I'll say it again, don't bet until you've done your homework." He laughed. "I was going to tell you a story about a bet a friend of mine at Trinity medical school made in the thirties in Dublin . . ."

Coleman called more odds and concluded, ". . . and the remaining twenty-one horses are at one hundred to one . . ."

"Including my little beauty, Crobeg." O'Reilly said, and lowered the volume. "Anyway Sean Barry was a County Corkman and a betting man . . ." He took another drink and shook his head, "I do believe Sean would have wagered on two snails crossing a path, but his great love was the horses. He and I were sitting in Davy Byrne's pub on Duke Street. Says he to me, 'Fingal, would you be willing to help me out?'

"'And what,' says I, 'would you like me to do?'

"'Could you lend me a fiver? It'll only be for about half an hour, so.'

"I confess I entertained a certain suspicion that an equine might be involved. 'And what's it for,' says I?"

"'There's a filly running in the third at Leopardstown this afternoon at a hundred to one.'" O'Reilly digressed to say, "Just like my Crobeg in the National," then continued, "Sean said, 'I really need the cash and a fiver on will bring one hundred and five back when she wins.'

" 'If she wins,' I said. 'If.' I've always made it an absolute that I don't mind lending money, but my father taught me never to lend more than I can afford to lose. You'll not always get the loan back. I shook my head. 'I would if I could, Sean, but I'm skint,' and I was. 'I've enough for a couple of pints and that's it.'

" 'Och well.' His face fell then he brightened and said, 'I think, bye, you could help me in another way, so.'

" 'Go on.'

"He pointed and said, 'This suit's brand-new. There's a pawn-broker's across the road. We'll go back to the gents. I'll take a cubicle, take off me suit, hand it over to you . . .'

" 'And you want me to pawn it?'

" 'I do and I'll wait in the cubicle for you to bring it back with my winnings.'

" 'You are nuts. I'll do no such thing.'

"Your man Sean Barry could have given Moses himself a run for his money in the 'soften Pharaoh's hard heart' stakes. Before you knew it I was in the gents, clutching a suit, in the pawn broker's, taking a fiver, and in the turf accountant's, placing a bet on a horse called Belfast Bombshell. . . . Hang on," he said and turned up the volume in time to hear, "They're under starter's orders."

I sighed. I wanted to know what happened to the Bombshell, but had to settle for, "And they're off. Freddie leads Red Tide by a nose. Both are ahead of the pack. They're coming to the first and yes, yes, Ayla's down. . . ." and there was a horse struggling to get back on its feet, its rider curled in a ball to avoid the hooves of the rest.

I must admit I'm not a horsey chap, but it was exciting to watch.

"Crobeg's up with the leaders," O'Reilly said, as every horse cleared the second hurdle.

David Coleman said, "There's trouble at the third. It's an open ditch fence."

The horses pounded up to it and soared over water and hedge, all but;

"And Ronald's Boy is down."

"Crobeg's not," I said, and now I was as caught up in the race as O'Reilly.

"After the fourth Red Tide's down and Culette has pulled up and refused, and so has Fearless Cavalier."

"Go on Crobeg, you-boy-yuh," O'Reilly said, hunching forward in his chair and cheering as no horses missed the fifth. "The next's Becher's Brook," he said. It's a real B. Four-foot-ten fence and an eight-foot brook."

I swear I was holding my breath.

The commentator said, "Jay Trump's over, followed by Freddie, Mr. Jones, the Rip . . . and, oh dear me, we have had a series of collisions. I can't tell who brought down whom, but Nedsmar's down and Ruby Glen, Sizzle On, Barley Croft, and one more. I can't make out which horse it is. . . ."

"Well I can, you bollix," said O'Reilly. "It's my horse." He took a deep breath. "Och well," he said, "we might as well enjoy the rest of the race," and we did to see just fourteen horses finish, with Freddie the favourite coming second and Jay Trump winning at one hundred to six.

"Fingal," I said, "you were telling me about your friend and his suit?"

O'Reilly snorted then said, "I'll put it this way. I didn't go back to Davy Byrne's for a couple of weeks in case Sean was still in there. I regret to say he hadn't really done his homework."

And we both laughed.

"You're in fine fettle, so," Kinky said, sticking her head round the door. From her kitchen below wafted the smells of kedgeree cooking and fresh bread cooling. "I'm pretty glad myself. Flo Bishop, Aggie Arbuthnot, Cissie Sloan, and me had six quid on Jay Trump, so."

"And," said O'Reilly, "did the sight help you, Kinky Kincaid?"

You do know that Kinky was fey.

She sniffed. "Not at all," she said. "That would be cheating. Flo got out the list of runners, and Aggie closed her eyes and stuck a pin it it."

"You what?" O'Reilly said. "I'll be damned."

The temptation to remark, "There's more than one way to do your homework," was almost overwhelming, but often times around Fingal Flahertie O'Reilly, as Falstaff might have said, "The better part of valour *is* discretion."

Sauces

AND

Jelly

Sauce Béarnaise

This is probably one of the most difficult of all the French sauces to make, but I think this recipe is quite foolproof. It is very good served with steak or fish.

Serves 2 to 4
6 egg yolks
2½ oz/75 ml white wine vinegar
7 oz/200 g butter, melted
1 Tbsp chopped fresh tarragon (or ½ tsp dried)
Salt and freshly ground black pepper.

First blend the egg yolks (I use the Sunbeam Mixmaster Doctor O'Reilly bought me). Then, with the mixer still running, add the vinegar very slowly and follow by gradually adding the butter. To finish, add the tarragon, season with salt and pepper, and serve immediately.

Hollandaise Sauce

Serves 4 to 6

3 eggs

2 Tbsp white wine vinegar

1 Tbsp lemon juice

Salt and freshly ground black pepper

4 oz/113 g butter

I do this in a blender but you may want to use a whisk. Separate the egg yolks and egg whites.

Heat the vinegar and lemon juice in a small saucepan and reduce to about half. Put the vinegar mixture into the blender and, with the blender running slowly, gradually add the egg yolks and salt and pepper. Melt the butter in the same pan that you used for the vinegar and with the blender still running add the melted butter to the egg yolk mixture. The sauce will start to thicken and if you think it is too thick just add a little hot water.

What you have now is a traditional Hollandaise sauce. I like to make more than I need so that I always have some in the freezer and am prepared to make a quick Benedict. However, the traditional Hollandaise does not freeze at all, so what you have to do is to beat up your leftover egg whites until they form soft peaks and fold them into the Hollandaise mixture. Freeze in individual portions and, when needed, just thaw and heat gently in a bain-marie or in a microwave on very low power for just a few seconds.

Kinky's Note:

As well as using this in my Eggs Benedict it is also delicious with steamed asparagus or fish dishes.

Easy Bread Sauce

Serves 4

1 onion, peeled

5 whole cloves

20 oz/590 ml milk

2 bay leaves

5 whole black peppercorns

4 oz/113 g fresh white bread crumbs

1½ oz/42 g butter

Salt and freshly ground black pepper

Stud the onion with the cloves so that it looks like a caveman's club, place in a saucepan with the milk, bay leaves, and peppercorns, and bring to the boil. Remove from the heat and let infuse for 15 to 20 minutes.

Discard the onion and bay leaves and fish out the peppercorns with a slotted spoon. Stir in the bread crumbs. Over a low heat cook this very gently for about 5 minutes, stirring now and again until the sauce has thickened and the bread crumbs have been incorporated. Stir in the butter and season with salt and pepper. Serve warm with Turkey with Stuffing and Gravy (page 331).

Kinky's Note:

Cloves are very strong-tasting so you really don't want to eat them. However, by studding the onion like this you just add the flavour. Lots of it.

Caper Sauce

Serves 4

2 oz/56 g butter

2 oz/56 g all-purpose flour

6 oz/180 ml lamb or vegetable stock

2 oz/60 ml whipping cream

Juice of ½ lemon

Salt and freshly ground black pepper

3 Tbsp capers, chopped

1 Tbsp chopped fresh parsley

Place the butter in a saucepan and cook gently until it just browns and smells slightly nutty. Remove from the heat and work in the flour. Return to the heat and cook for a minute, then add the lamb stock, whisk in the cream and lemon juice, and season with salt and pepper. Simmer gently for about 5 minutes and add the capers and parsley.

Serve with chicken, fish, or Roast Rack of Lamb (page 159).

Kinky's Note:

This method of making sauce is the classic French way. The act of melting butter and stirring an equal quantity of flour into it is called making a roux (pronounced "roo") and can be the basis for many sauces. It is a good idea to make more roux than you need, as it will keep wrapped in film or foil in the refrigerator. However, the rule is that if your roux is warm you whisk a cold liquid into it. If the roux is cold you whisk in warm liquid.

Red Wine Sauce

Serves 3 to 4

2 shallots, finely chopped

1 garlic clove, grated or finely crushed

1 tsp olive oil

8 oz/235 ml pinot noir or other red wine (not full-bodied)

8 oz/235 ml chicken stock or beef stock

3 oz/85 g butter, cubed

Salt and freshly ground black pepper

1 tsp brown sugar (optional)

1 tsp chopped fresh thyme (optional)

Sweat the shallots and garlic in the olive oil, add the red wine, and cook for a very few minutes. Now add the stock and bring to the boil. Continue to cook until reduced by half. Strain into a saucepan and bring to a simmer. Whisk the cubed butter in gradually, one piece at a time. The sauce will become thick and glossy. Season with salt and pepper to taste and add the sugar (if using). Finally, stir in the thyme (if using).

Serve with steak or other red meat.

Port and Redcurrant Sauce

Serves 4

1 tsp olive oil

3 shallots, finely chopped

3 oz/85 g butter, cubed

8 oz/235 ml chicken stock

6 oz/170 g redcurrants

6 oz/180 ml port or red wine

1 tsp brown sugar (optional)

Salt and freshly ground black pepper

Heat the oil in a large frying pan, add the shallots, and cook gently for a few minutes without allowing them to burn. You may need to add a knob of butter. Add the chicken stock and redcurrants and cook until the fruit is soft. Pour and push the sauce through a fine-mesh sieve into a clean pan, add the port, and bring to a brisk boil. Reduce the liquid by almost half and whisk in the remaining butter. Add the sugar (if using) and season with salt and pepper to taste.

Serve with chicken, duck, pork, or turkey.

Cranberry Sauce

Serves 6
9 oz/255 g fresh or frozen cranberries
3½ oz/105 ml white wine
3½ oz/100 g sugar, plus extra as needed
1 tsp grated orange zest
Lemon juice (optional)

Combine all the ingredients in a saucepan. Bring to the boil and simmer gently for 10 minutes. Stir with a wooden spoon, thus helping to burst some of the berries. Taste and add more sugar or lemon juice if necessary. Serve warm with turkey or pork.

Redcurrant Jelly

Makes 2 16-oz/475-ml jars
2 lb/910 g redcurrants
2 lb/910 g sugar, warmed

Sterilise two 16-ounce/475-ml jars.

Place the redcurrants in a large saucepan or preserving pan and bring slowly to the boil. Stir and press the redcurrants to break down the fruit and release the juice. Cook for about 10 minutes, then add the warmed sugar and stir until dissolved. Bring the mixture to a rapid boil and boil for about 10 minutes. Test for setting point by dropping a teaspoonful onto a chilled plate, leave it to cool for a few minutes, then push it with your finger. If a crinkly skin has formed on the top of the jam it has set. Or you can use a sugar thermometer clipped to the side of the pan and when the temperature reaches 220°F/104°C, the setting point should be reached.

Now you can use either a jelly bag or a sieve lined with gauze placed over a bowl. Pour the jelly mixture into it and let it drip through. If you don't mind not having a completely clear jelly, you can press to extract as much juice as possible. Pour the juice into the sterilized jars and cover. The process is exactly the same for a larger quantity.

Frockton
(Bilberry or Blueberry) Jelly

Makes 2 16-oz/475-ml mason jars

2 lb/910 g bilberries or blueberries

2 lb/910 g sugar, warmed

Place a small plate in the refrigerator to chill. Place the blueberries in a large saucepan and bring slowly to the boil. Stir and press the blueberries to break down the fruit and release the juice. Cook for about 10 minutes, then add the warmed sugar and stir until dissolved. Bring the mixture to a rapid boil and boil for about 10 minutes. Test for setting point by dropping a little on the cold plate. If a skin has formed when you push the jam with your finger it has reached setting point. Or you could test with a sugar (candy) thermometer clipped to the side of the pan. Setting point should be reached at 220°F/104°C. If it is still too runny, bring it back to the boil and cook until it thickens. If you hold a wooden spoon up and the jelly clings to the spoon, then it is ready to set.

Now you can either use a jelly bag or a sieve lined with gauze placed over a bowl. Pour the jelly mixture into it and let it drip through. If you don't mind not having a completely clear jelly, you can press to extract as much juice as possible. Pour the juice into two warmed 16-ounce/475-ml jars and cover. Keep refrigerated.

The process is exactly the same for a larger quantity. Just be sure that setting point has been reached before transferring to the warmed jars.

Crème Anglaise

Serves 2 to 4

5 oz/150 ml milk

5 oz/150 ml heavy cream

4 egg yolks

1½ oz/42 g sugar

Heat the milk and cream in a medium saucepan until just at a boil. Remove from the heat. Whisk the egg yolks and sugar in a bowl until pale and creamy. Gradually add the hot milk, just a little at a time to the egg yolk mixture, whisking until all has been incorporated. Pour the egg and milk mix back into the saucepan and bring to a simmer. Keeping the pan at just a simmer, cook for 3 to 4 minutes or until the mixture has thickened.

Lemon Curd

Makes 3 or 4 8-oz/235-ml jars, depending on how juicy the lemons are

Grated zest and juice of 4 unwaxed lemons

7 oz/200 g sugar

3½ oz/100 g butter

3 eggs, separated, plus 1 egg yolk

Sterilise four 8-ounce/235-ml jars.

Put the lemon zest and juice in a large bowl. Set the bowl in a saucepan of simmering water, making sure the bottom of the bowl does not touch the water. Add the sugar and butter and stir around until the butter has melted and the sugar has dissolved. In a separate bowl, whisk the egg whites and add the yolks. Then beat this into the lemon mixture and cook, stirring occasionally, for about 15 minutes. By this time the lemon curd should have thickened but if it has not, just give it a few more minutes. Pour into the prepared jars and allow it to cool before putting on the lids. Store in the refrigerator.

VARIATION

Lime or Orange Curd. Try limes or Seville oranges instead.

Kinky's Note:

If you microwave the lemon halves for 10 to 15 seconds each the yield of juice is almost doubled.

Brandy Sauce

Serves 6 to 8 with Christmas Pudding

2 oz/56 g unsalted butter

2 oz/56 g all-purpose flour

20 oz/590 ml milk

2 oz/60 ml brandy

2 oz/56 g superfine sugar

Melt the butter in a medium saucepan over a medium heat and stir in the flour. Cook for 2 minutes and gradually stir in the milk. Bring to the boil, stirring all the time. Simmer gently for 10 minutes. Stir in the brandy and sugar. Serve warm with Christmas Pudding (page 342).

Mint Sauce

Serves 4

4 Tbsp fresh mint leaves

2 oz/60 ml boiling water

1 Tbsp sugar, plus extra as needed

A pinch of salt

2 oz/60 ml white wine vinegar, plus extra as needed

Finely chop the mint, or process in a blender. Place it in a small bowl, and stir in the boiling water, sugar, and salt. Add the vinegar and allow the sauce to cool. Taste and add more water, salt, or vinegar as necessary.

Serve with lamb.

Any
Port in a...

'you know, Barry," O'Reilly said, as late on a February Friday afternoon we turned a corner in Belfast heading toward the Crown Liquor Saloon, "We've taken a quick right from the Grosvenor Road, and now we are on Great Victoria Street."

We'd been at a refresher lecture for GPs at the Royal Victoria Hospital.

"It's always an excellent idea to know *exactly* where you are at all times."

Yet another pithy aphorism from O'Reilly's limitless store of truisms that included, as air travel was now becoming an established fact of life, "Turbulence is inevitably stimulated when the stewardess serves coffee." I filed "knowing where you are" under "try to forget it," but in a very short time it would be brought back to mind in a most forceful way. Bear with me. Like anything to do with my old mentor, explaining may take a little time.

We entered the venerable old pub that Sir John Betjeman had called his favourite, found a vacant booth, and sat on leather-covered benches. The place was still in all its glory after its refurbishment in 1885. Dark wood-panelled half walls were topped by engraved glass inserts adorned with incised bunches of grapes. Tobacco smoke wreathed upward through air redolent of beer and spirit fumes. Conversations rose and fell, punctuated by the clink of glass on glass.

"Pint?" said O'Reilly.

He was clearly in an expansive mood.

"Please," I said, and after the requisite passage of time that it takes for a good pint of Guinness to be poured and allowed to settle, two straight glasses of the black stuff crowned with creamy heads duly appeared.

"Thanks," O'Reilly said to the waiter and paid. *"Sláinte."*

"Cheers," I said and drank.

"Do you know what's going to happen tomorrow, Barry?" he asked.

I hesitated before answering. He'd used that lead-in before—usually before he asked me for a favour. Eventually I managed a guarded, "No."

"Ireland are playing Scotland at rugby at Murrayfield in Edinburgh." He drank.

"Good for them," I said and I must confess I was not particularly a fan of the game, but I have probably told you that among his other attributes, the redoubtable Doctor Fingal Flahertie O'Reilly had, in his youth, represented his country playing the manly game of rugby football. It is not a contest for the faint of heart. Even in O'Reilly's fifties he was still an avid follower of the sport.

"I think Ireland should have a very good chance. Ken Kennedy and Roger Young are two Ulstermen on the team."

"I know them both," I said. "Young read dentistry and Kennedy medicine at Queen's when I was there." And I wished them and the rest of the side well. A schoolboy, William Webb Ellis at England's Rugby Public School, is credited with picking up the ball and running with it in the mid-nineteenth century and thus inventing the game. However, there is a body of opinion that it was discovered in 1211 by a member of Temüjin's (if you prefer, Genghis Khan's) Golden Horde. Of course in lieu of a ball the old Mongol was carrying the head of an opposing player from the Jin Dynasty's recently defeated army.

The modern game and its North American counterparts are perhaps a little gentler—perhaps, although our transatlantic cousins do take the precaution of wearing helmets and body armour. "Will it be on the telly?" I asked, thinking I'd twigged to the upcoming favour. I was off call tonight and tomorrow. I could hear his mental gears grinding. I was going to be asked to cover tomorrow afternoon. And I had plans.

"I don't suppose . . ."

Here it comes.

"You'd cover me tonight?"

"Tonight? I thought the game was on tomorrow."

"It is, but most of my friends who follow Irish fortunes, including Charlie Greer who played for Ireland, are going over to support the team."

"And you want to go too?" He'd be asking for three days cover if that was the case.

He shook his big shaggy head. "Just this evening," he said. "You see there's a crowd going over tonight on the ferry. Coach from Belfast to Larne, cross the channel to Cairnryan overnight, and the coach takes them to Edinburgh in the morning."

In those safer days before hijacking became an even rougher sport than rugby, friends and family often accompanied travellers on board and had a glass or two before the vessel sailed. "And you want to go and have a jar on board with them?"

He beamed with such intensity I swear it dimmed the house lights for a moment. "I knew the day I took you on I was hiring a man of great perspicacity. . . ."

"Flattery will get you nowhere," was not one of his originals like "know where you are," but it had a ring of truth to it.

"You see," he said, "I thought if I ran you to the Queen's Quay station you could get the train to Ballybucklebo. I could nip down to Larne, go aboard and have a few jars with my pals, then drive home." The big man was like a six-year-old begging to open one, just one present, on Christmas Eve.

I laughed. "Very well," I said.

O'Reilly said, "I'll make it up to you, Barry. Thanks a million."

To cut a long story short, we finished our pints and drove to the station, where I was duly deposited before O'Reilly took off for Larne.

Medically, my night was uneventful, but there was no sign of O'Reilly at breakfast. I thought he'd probably had fun the night before and was sleeping late, but I knew he'd be furious that he'd missed the grilled kippers—smoked herring from the fishing village of Ardglass—I'd relished.

The phone rang in the hall. Kinky answered and came in. "Doctor Laverty," she said, looking puzzled, "it does be himself to speak with you, so."

I rose and frowned. O'Reilly was on the phone?

"Hello, Laverty here."

"Barry," O'Reilly's voice came over the wire. Was there a hint of contriteness? "Barry, please stay on call until I get home."

Get home? "Where are you?"

There was a long pause before the voice said, "In a hotel at Cairnryan in Scotland. I forgot to get off the ferry in Larne before it sailed."

I should have been angry, but I had to laugh and I could not resist saying, "Thank you, Fingal."

"What for?"

"You were right to teach me that yesterday. It is an excellent idea to know *exactly* where you are. Cairnryan. Ye gods."

And I will say in fairness to the big-hearted man, a chuckle came over the wire.

DESSERTS

Puddings

Sure hasn't Doctor O'Reilly got a very sweet tooth and amn't I having my work cut out to give him nice puddings? When I was a girl almost every pudding, for isn't that what we called them, was accompanied by custard made from Bird's custard powder. Usually apples, which were so plentiful, were involved too, and apple tart was probably on the plate most weeks. The other nursery puddings often served (too often) were tapioca and sago made with milk and were a means of getting us children to get all the nutrients we needed for strong bones. (For those of you who never had to endure the tapioca pudding—known to us as frogspawn—it looked rather like a round form of rice but was made from the cassava plant, grown in Brazil.) I hope I have given you something a little more adventurous as well as some old favourites.

Apple and Bread-Crumb Pudding

Serves 4

4 oz/113 g butter, plus extra as needed

1 lb 2 oz/500 g tart apples, peeled, cored, and thinly sliced

9 oz/255 g bread crumbs (made from stale bread, crusts removed)

A pinch of ground cinnamon

2 eggs

8 oz/235 ml milk

2½ oz/70 g sugar

A pinch of salt

Preheat the oven to 325°F/170°C. Lightly butter a 1 quart/960 ml gratin dish.

Melt half of the butter in a large frying pan, add the apples, and cook, stirring and turning over a low heat, until quite tender. Cook the bread crumbs in a separate pan with the rest of the butter, stirring regularly over a low heat, until crisp and golden. Do add more butter if you need to. Spread the crumbs into the buttered gratin dish. Place the apples on the crumbs and sprinkle cinnamon on top. Whisk together the eggs, milk, sugar, and salt and pour gently over the apples. Bake for an hour and serve with cream.

Kinky's Note:

Whilst Bramley apples would have been the cooking apples of choice in Ulster, if they are not available, try using Braeburn or any other slightly tart variety.

Caramelized Armagh Apple and Cinnamon Brûlée

This beautiful dish was given to me by Paul McKnight, the executive chef of the Culloden Hotel. Culloden Estate and Spa, 1 Bangor Road, Holywood. Co Down. N Ireland.

Makes 6

APPLE COMPOTE
3½ oz/100 g butter
3 large Armagh cooking apples, peeled, cored, and diced
3½ oz/100 g brown sugar
Ground cinnamon

BRÛLÉE
17 oz/505 ml whipping cream
1 vanilla pod
4½ oz/127 g egg yolks (about 6 yolks)
2¼ oz/63 g granulated sugar, plus extra for topping
Ground cinnamon

Preheat the oven to 250°F/130°C.

FOR THE APPLE COMPOTE:
Melt the butter in a pan over a medium heat, add the apples, sugar, and cinnamon, and cook until caramelized in colour and flavour. Place the caramelized apples in the bottom of six ramekins.

FOR THE BRÛLÉE:

Bring the cream and vanilla pod to the boil. Whisk the egg yolks and sugar together in a bowl, pour the boiled cream into the egg mixture, and whisk. Pour through a sieve into a jug. Fill each ramekin with brûlée mix to three-quarters full. Bake for 15 minutes. You are looking for a slight wobble when cooked. Chill until needed. Top each ramekin with a sprinkling of sugar and cinnamon and caramelize using a blowtorch. Serve.

Kinky's Note:

Armagh apples are usually Bramley. If they are not available try using Braeburn or any other slightly tart variety.

Chocolate Mousse

Serves 6

8 oz/227 g good-quality dark chocolate (at least 70% cocoa)

2½ oz/75 ml water

1 oz/56 g unsalted butter, at room temperature and softened slightly

1 Tbsp crème fraîche or sour cream

5 eggs, separated, at room temperature

A pinch of salt

1 Tbsp sugar

Melt the chocolate with the water in a large bowl over a saucepan of simmering water, stirring until it has melted. Don't let the chocolate become too hot. Stir in the softened butter and crème fraîche. Remove the bowl from the heat and, using an electric mixer, beat in the egg yolks one at a time. Using clean beaters in a separate bowl, beat the egg whites with the salt until they are just foamy. Increase the mixer speed, add the sugar, and beat until stiff. Now gradually fold the egg white mixture into the chocolate and transfer to individual ramekins or a serving bowl. Cover and chill in the refrigerator for 24 hours before serving.

VARIATION

Add peppermint extract or rum to taste.

Chocolate Pots

Serves 8

8 oz/227 g sugar

17 oz/505 ml whole milk

8 oz/227 g good-quality chocolate, at least 70% cocoa, broken into pieces

8 egg yolks plus 1 egg

4 oz/120 ml whipping cream

A few mint leaves for decoration

Preheat the oven 350°F/180°C. Dissolve the sugar in the milk in a large saucepan and bring to the boil. Now stir in the pieces of chocolate and bring back to the boil, stirring all the time. Whisk the egg yolks and then the whole egg together and gradually whisk this into the chocolate mixture. Pour into eight 4-ounce/120-ml pots or ramekins. Set the pots in a baking dish and fill the dish with enough hot water to come halfway up the outside of the pots. Bake for about 30 minutes, by which time the chocolate will have set. Allow the pots to cool and then refrigerate until cold. When ready to serve, whip the cream and then spoon some on top of each pot and decorate with a mint leaf.

Kinky's Note:

This method of cooking by setting the pots inside another *container* of boiling water is often referred to as a bain-marie.

Coffee Ice Cream

Serves 6

17 oz/505 ml heavy cream

10 oz/284 g sweetened condensed milk

1½ Tbsp espresso coffee powder or strong brewed coffee

2 Tbsp Tia Maria or Kahlua

Dark chocolate, grated

Using a food processor or an electric mixer beat the cream until thick. Add the condensed milk, coffee, and liqueur and continue to beat until thick. Transfer to a lidded plastic container and freeze. Serve in individual glass bowls decorated with grated chocolate.

Crème Brûlée

Serves 4

16 oz/475 ml heavy cream

2 oz/60 ml whole milk

1 tsp vanilla extract or the seeds from 2 vanilla pods

5 egg yolks

4 oz/113 g brown sugar

Preheat the oven to 300°F/150°C. Pour the cream and milk into a heavy-bottomed saucepan and bring to almost a simmer, ever so gently. Add the vanilla to the mixture and give it a good stir round. Whisk in the egg yolks and 2½ ounces/70 g of the sugar and pour the mixture into four 6-oz individual ramekins. (If you don't have time to finish them now you can pop them into the fridge and finish them later.)

Set the ramekins in a baking dish and fill the dish with enough hot water to come halfway up the outside of the ramekins. (This is called a bain-marie. Himself explained that this was used in an early form of chemical science to heat things very slowly and gently. But I digress . . .) Now cook the custard for 30 to 35 minutes, until set, then allow to cool. You can leave them in the fridge if you do not need to serve them immediately.

Now for the topping. Sprinkle the remaining 1½ ounces/43 g sugar on top of each dish and caramelize it using a blowtorch or under a hot broiler. I just love to use my blowtorch that Emer Cullen brought me from London. You remember Emer used to work at the Café de Paris there, before she came here to work for the Marquis's father. However if you don't have one you can brown them under a hot grill or broiler.

Kinky's Note:

The leftover egg whites can be frozen or refrigerated for later use. You could make a simple Pavlova (page 275) or try the Eton Mess (page 269), which I think is more unusual and simply delicious.

Eton Mess

Dear Doctor O'Reilly with his sweet tooth just loves this dessert. He tells me that it may have been invented by a dog knocking over a picnic basket at a cricket match in the grounds of Eton, one of England's most prestigious schools, but that's another story. This looks very pretty layered in a glass bowl and works equally well with rhubarb or plums.

The secret for successful meringue is to make sure that not a single drop of egg yolk gets into the mixture and to ensure that your bowl and beaters are perfectly clean and grease-free. I rub a splash of vinegar on a paper towel round the bowl and beaters.

Serves 8

MERINGUE
5 egg whites
10 oz/284 g superfine sugar
1 tsp cornstarch
1 tsp vinegar

MESS
8 oz/227 g strawberries, hulled
8 oz/227 g raspberries
2 tsp sugar
2 tsp balsamic vinegar
16 oz/475 ml whipping cream or heavy cream (or use a mixture of cream and crème fraîche)
2 tsp vanilla extract

FOR THE MERINGUE:

Preheat the oven to 325°F/160°C. Grease an 18- by 12-inch baking sheet and dust it with flour. (This stops the meringue from spreading.) Using an electric mixer, whisk the egg whites just long enough to see them turn a greenish colour, then, still beating, add one-third of the sugar and continue beating for another couple of minutes before adding the next third. Beat again and add the rest of the sugar. Now you should beat until it's as stiff and glossy as can be and then add the cornstarch and vinegar. Spread the mixture evenly on the baking sheet and bake it for 45 minutes, then turn the oven off and leave the meringue in for 30 minutes.

FOR THE MESS:

Reserve a few whole berries for decoration. Slice half the strawberries, place in a bowl, and add half the raspberries and the sugar. Mash the fruit, add the vinegar, and let marinate. Whip the cream with the vanilla until stiff. Fill a 2-quart/2-L glass serving dish with alternating layers of cream, pieces of meringue, and mashed and whole fruit. Decorate the top with the reserved whole berries and serve.

PLUM OR RHUBARB ETON MESS

Make the meringue as above in Eton Mess.

> **MESS**
>
> 1 lb/455 g plums, pitted and sliced, or rhubarb, chopped
> 2 Tbsp water
> 2 Tbsp sugar
> 16 oz/475 ml heavy cream or a mixture of cream and crème fraîche

Cook the fruit in a stainless-steel or enamel saucepan with the water until soft. Add the sugar and stir until dissolved. Whip the cream until stiff. Proceed as before, layering the meringue with the whipped cream and the rhubarb in a large serving bowl.

Lemon Pots

Serves 6 to 8

15 oz/445 ml heavy cream

4½ oz/127 g sugar

Grated zest and juice of 2 lemons

Raspberries (optional)

Combine all the ingredients in a saucepan and bring to the boil, stirring. Allow to bubble for exactly 5 minutes. Remove the pan from the heat and leave to infuse for 30 minutes. Strain the mixture into a jug and pour it into six-to-eight 2-oz ramekins or espresso coffee cups. Refrigerate for at least 12 hours, decorate with a few raspberries (if desired), and serve.

Marmalade Pudding

Serves 6 to 8

8 oz/227 g all-purpose flour

1 tsp baking powder

½ tsp baking soda

9 oz/255g butter

2½ oz/70 g superfine sugar

2½ oz/70 g brown sugar

5 oz/142 g orange marmalade

4 eggs

Grated zest and juice of 1 orange, mixed together

Preheat the oven to 350°F/180°C. Butter a 10-inch/25-cm square baking dish.

Sift the flour, baking powder, and baking soda together. Cream the butter and sugars and beat in the marmalade. Add the eggs one at a time. After each addition beat in a little of the sifted flour and finally add half the orange juice mixture. Put the batter in the baking dish and smooth the top. Bake for about 40 minutes, until the pudding has risen and the top is light brown. (Keep a careful eye on it.) Brush the top with the remaining juice mixture and serve with custard or cream.

Kinky's Note:

To prevent a creamed butter and sugar mixture from curdling when adding eggs, just add a little flour and beat it in after each egg.

Orange and Chocolate Soufflé

Serves 4 to 6

2½ tsp unflavored gelatin

Grated zest and juice of 1 large orange, plus orange segments for garnish

5 eggs

3 oz/85 g sugar

7 oz/200 g plain dark chocolate, at least 70% cocoa, chopped, plus grated
   chocolate for garnish

2 oz/60 ml water

3 oz/90 ml heavy cream

Sprinkle the gelatin over the orange juice and set aside to soften. Separate two of the eggs and place their whites in a bowl to use later. Put the yolks, the remaining eggs, and the sugar in a large bowl and set it over a saucepan of simmering water. Whisk the mixture for about 10 minutes, until it becomes thick and creamy, then set aside. Place the chocolate into a third bowl, add the water, and set it over the pan of simmering water. Stir until the chocolate has melted and become smooth and runny and add the orange zest. Allow to cool.

While the chocolate cools, beat the two egg whites until quite stiff. In a separate bowl, whip the cream until stiff. By now the chocolate mixture should have cooled down. If it has not, place the bowl in a larger bowl of cold water and stir the chocolate around. When it is cold, stir and fold the chocolate and the orange juice mixture into the egg and sugar mixture. Now fold the egg whites and whipped cream carefully through the chocolate and egg mixture. Pour into a 2 qt/2 L glass serving dish and refrigerate for 2 to 3 hours. Decorate with orange segments and grated chocolate and serve.

Pavlova

The secret for successful meringue is to make sure that not a single drop of egg yolk gets into the mixture. To ensure that my bowl and beaters are perfectly clean and grease-free I rub a splash of vinegar on a paper towel round the bowl and beaters.

Serves 4 to 6
3 egg whites
6 oz/170 g white sugar
1 tsp cornstarch
1 tsp vinegar
8 oz/227 g strawberries, hulled and sliced, or raspberries
8 oz/235 ml heavy cream

Preheat the oven to 325°F/160°C. Grease a baking sheet and dust lightly with flour. (This stops the meringue from spreading.)

Using an electric mixer, whisk the egg whites just long enough to see them turn a greenish colour then, still beating, add one-third of the sugar and continue beating for another minute before adding the next third. Beat again and add the rest of the sugar. Now you should beat until it's as stiff and glossy as can be and then add the cornstarch and vinegar. Place the meringue, shaped to fit your serving plate, on the baking sheet. Bake it for 45 minutes, then turn the oven off and leave the meringue in for 30 minutes. Turn upside down onto a serving plate and allow to cool. This will create an indented shape in which to put the filling.

Whip the cream until stiff and cover the top of the pavlova. Decorate with raspberries or strawberries and whipped cream.

VARIATION

Spread the meringue with Lemon Curd (page 245) before covering it with whipped cream. Decorate with raspberries.

Queen of Puddings
(Bread and Butter Pudding)

Apparently, Queen of Puddings dates back to the seventeenth century; this may have been the original recipe from the Closet of Sir Kenelm Digby.

AN EXCELLENT BAKED PUDDING

Slice thin two peny-roles, or one, of French-bread, the tender part. Lay it in a dish or pan. Pour upon it a quart of Cream, that hath been well boiled. Let it stand almost half an hour, till it be almost cold. Then stir the bread and Cream very well together, till the bread be well broken and Incorporated. (If you have no French bread, take stale Kingston bread, grated) add to this two spoonfuls of fine Wheat-flower, the yolks of four Eggs, and the whites of two; a Nutmeg—grated small; Sugar to your taste; a little Salt, and the Marrow of two bones a little shredded. Stir all these together; then pour it into a dish greased over with Butter, and set it uncovered in the Oven to bake. About half an hour will serve, and give the top a yellow crispiness. Before you put in the Marrow, put in a quarter of a pound and a half of Raisins of the Sun, and as much of Currants; Ordering them so, that they may not fall to the bottom, but be all about the pudding.

Sure I don't think that Doctor O'Reilly would like me to put marrow in his Queen of puddings but I never got round to asking him.

Serves 6
4 oz/113 g butter, softened
8–10 slices white bread
3½ oz/100 g raisins
Grated zest of 1 lemon
9 oz/265 ml milk

4½ oz/135 ml heavy cream, plus extra for serving

3½ oz/100 g sugar

3 eggs, separated

Preheat the oven to 350°F/180°C. Butter a 9 by 7 by 2-inch/23 by 18- by 5-cm baking dish.

Butter the bread and arrange in layers in the baking dish, sprinkling each layer with the raisins and lemon zest. Then whisk the egg yolks and one of the egg whites in a bowl with the milk, cream, and half of the sugar and pour this over the layers of bread. Bake for 30 minutes or until set and remove from the oven.

Now beat the two remaining egg whites until stiff and whisk in the rest of the sugar. Cover the top of the pudding with this meringue mixture and return to the oven for a further 10 to 15 minutes or until the top is golden. Serve warm with cream or crème fraîche.

VARIATIONS

You could use Barmbrack (page 87) and omit the raisins, or spread the buttered bread with marmalade and omit the lemon zest and raisins.

For a savoury pudding you can omit the meringue topping, raisins, and lemon zest and add about 6 oz/170 g grated cheese between the layers and on top.

Rhubarb Fool

Miss Nolan, who is just back from a teacher exchange visit to France, tells me that she thinks the word "fool" might come from a French word meaning to crush or puree.

Serves 4 to 6

RHUBARB
1 lb/455 g rhubarb, cut into 1-in/2.5-cm pieces
2 Tbsp water
1 (½-in/12-mm) piece fresh ginger, grated
4 oz/113 g sugar

CRÈME ANGLAISE
5 oz/150 ml milk
5 oz/150 ml heavy cream
4 egg yolks
1½ oz/42 g sugar

FOR THE RHUBARB:
Put the rhubarb, water, and ginger in an enamel or stainless-steel saucepan, cover, and cook over a very gentle heat until soft. This should take about 30 minutes. Add the sugar and stir until dissolved. Refrigerate until ready to assemble.

FOR THE CRÈME ANGLAISE:
Heat the milk and cream in a saucepan until just at a boil. Remove from the heat. Whisk the egg yolks and sugar in a bowl until pale and creamy. Gradually add the hot milk to the egg yolk mixture, whisking all the time, until incorporated. Return the mixture to the saucepan and bring to a simmer. Keeping the pan at just a simmer, cook for 3 to

4 minutes or until the mixture has thickened. Refrigerate until cold. Layer the rhubarb and crème anglaise in four to six tall sundae glasses and serve with Ginger Biscuits (page 301) on the side.

Kinky's Note:

If you are in a hurry you might prefer to use thick Greek yogurt instead of crème anglaise.

Oeufs à la Neige
(Eggs in Snow)

Ma used to make this for special occasions and I loved it. On reflection, I think it was a very nutritious pudding for growing children and it is also appealing to the eye, as it really does look like eggs in snow or floating islands. (The French have a similar recipe called *île flottante* or "floating island.")

The secret for successful meringue is to make sure that not a single drop of egg yolk gets into the mixture and to ensure that your bowl and beaters are perfectly clean and grease-free. I rub a splash of vinegar on a paper towel round the bowl and beaters.

Serves 4

EGGS
4 egg whites (reserve the yolks for the "snow")
A pinch of salt
7½ oz/214 g sugar
7 oz/210 ml milk

SNOW
1 tsp vanilla extract
5 oz/150 ml heavy cream
4 egg yolks
1½ oz/42 g sugar

FOR THE EGGS:

Using an electric mixer, whisk the egg whites and salt just long enough to see them turn a greenish colour then, still beating, add one-third of the sugar and continue beating for another minute before adding the next third. Beat again and add the rest of the sugar. Now you should beat until it's as stiff and glossy as can be.

Pour the milk and cream into a medium saucepan and bring to a simmer. Using a tablespoon, scoop spoonfuls of meringue and carefully poach them for a minute or two on both sides in the milk. (Don't try to do too many at a time, as you need to leave room for the meringue to expand.) Using a slotted spoon, remove the meringue "eggs" and set aside in a serving dish. Reserve the milk and cream mixture.

FOR THE SNOW:

Add the vanilla to the saucepan with the milk and cream and bring to the boil, then remove from the heat. Whisk the egg yolks with the sugar in a bowl until pale and creamy. Slowly pour this into the milk mixture, whisking all the time. Return to a very low heat and stir constantly with a wooden spoon until the sauce thickens and coats the side of the spoon. Do not let it boil. Remove from the heat and pour around, not over, the "eggs" in the serving dish. Chill before serving.

Sticky Toffee Pudding

Serves 6 to 8

PUDDING

2 oz/56 g butter, softened

6 oz/170 g demerara or brown sugar

2 eggs

7½ oz/214 g self-rising flour

2 Tbsp molasses or treacle

1 Tbsp golden or maple syrup

7 oz/200 g pitted dates, chopped

10 oz/295 ml boiling water

1 tsp baking soda

TOFFEE SAUCE

4 oz/120 ml whipping cream

2 oz/56 g butter

2 oz/56 g dark muscovado or dark brown sugar

2 Tbsp molasses or treacle

1 Tbsp maple syrup or golden syrup

FOR THE PUDDING:

Preheat the oven to 400°F/200°C. Grease and flour an 8-inch/20-cm square baking dish or six-to-eight individual muffin pans.

Beat the butter and sugar together until pale and fluffy. Beat in the eggs gradually and add a little flour (to stop the mixture from curdling). Add the molasses and syrup and finally fold in the rest of the flour. Add the dates to the boiling water and stir in the baking soda. Add this quickly to the prepared pudding mixture and pour into the baking dish or muffin pans. Bake for 20 to 25 minutes, until the pudding is well risen and springy to the touch.

FOR THE TOFFEE SAUCE:

While the pudding is cooking, put all the sauce ingredients in a saucepan over a low heat and bring to the boil. Serve the pudding on individual plates with the sauce poured over the top.

Strawberry or Raspberry Ice Cream

Serves 6

17 oz/505 ml whipping cream

1 (14-oz/400-g) can low-fat sweetened condensed milk

1 tsp vanilla extract

8 oz/235 ml strawberry or raspberry yogurt

8 oz/227 g strawberries, hulled and sliced, or raspberries

1 Tbsp confectioners' sugar

Line a 9 by 5-inch/23 by 12-cm loaf tin with cling film. Using an electric mixer or a food processor, beat the cream in a large bowl, add the condensed milk and vanilla, and continue to beat for about 10 minutes, until thick. Fold in the yogurt. Mash the fruit with the sugar and fold through the ice cream mixture. Pour into the loaf tin or a lidded plastic container, such as Tupperware, and freeze until firm. Serve sliced, with fruit to garnish.

Kinky's Note:

Evaporated milk is unsweetened and is milk which has had about 60 percent of the water removed via evaporation. Condensed milk, usually called sweetened condensed milk, has also had 60 percent of its water removed, but the difference is that sugar has been added. "Unsweetened condensed milk" is a redundant term: it is simply evaporated milk.

VARIATIONS

Substitute chocolate chips and mint extract for the fruit and omit the yogurt. Or try it with broken honeycomb instead of the fruit.

A Matter of Chutzpah

Now there's a word, Barry," O'Reilly said to me, looking up from his book. "*Chutzpah*. Chutzpah."

"Never heard of it," I said from my armchair in the big upstairs lounge. "Is it Irish? What does it mean?"

"It's Yiddish, I believe," he said, sipping his Jameson, "and I think here in Ulster we'd say 'gall,' or 'quare brass neck,' you know, absolute disregard for ordinary conventions. Cheek. Impertinence, but they're not quite accurate. There's often a humorous aspect to it."

I sipped my sherry. "You mean like the time Donal Donnelly let his racing greyhound Bluebird drink a belly full of water before every race to slow her down so the odds on her got longer and longer and then when he wanted her to win he didn't give her a drink and when she had won and was drug tested nothing showed up?"

"Close," said O'Reilly, "but I'm not sure it exactly captures the whole flavour. At least not as I understand it." He rose, walked over to the big bay window, stared out over the rooftops of Bally-bucklebo, turned, and as he walked back said, "It's more like a fellah up on a reckless driving charge who appears an hour late in court and asks the judge's indulgence because your man had had to walk because on his way to court—he'd crashed his car."

I chuckled and said, "I see what you mean."

"Och," he said, "it's still not quite right. I think I've a better example. From my days as a medical student at Trinity in Dublin."

As he went to the sideboard to refresh his whiskey, I steeled myself for another (while we were on the subject of foreign words) trek or safari down the labyrinthine byways of his vast memory.

The door opened.

I greeted Kinky's appearance bearing a loaded tray with the enthusiasm of Baden-Powell for the forces relieving Mafeking in May 1900. Perhaps we could let the subject of chutzpah drop.

Kinky said, "I did make up a light plate, so." She pointed and said, "That does be my chicken liver pâté on wheaten bread, and that is my smoked mackerel pâté on melba toast."

"Thank you, Kinky," O'Reilly said as she left. "Come on Barry, tuck in." He loaded a side plate and went back to his chair. I followed suit. The chicken liver pâté simply melted in my mouth.

O'Reilly mumbled through a mouthful of smoked mackerel, "I was telling you about chutzpah . . ."

Oh well. The snack would make listening a bit easier.

"Did you ever go to watch Ireland play rugby football?" he asked, returning and taking his seat.

"Yes, actually. When I was a student. Back in 1963. Jack Mills and I saw Ireland play England at Lansdowne Road."

"Begob," said O'Reilly, "I was at that game too. With Charlie Greer . . ."

I knew that he and Mister Greer, now a highly reputed neurosurgeon at the Royal Victoria Hospital, had played together in the '30s representing Ireland. It had been one of the proudest moments of the big man's life.

"Not much of a match. Scoreless draw, but we got our own back next year we beat them eighteen to five at Twickenham in England." His grin was feral. I suspected that O'Reilly, like many of the international rugby-watching fraternity be they Irish, Welsh, Scottish, or French, not only supported his own country in the Five Nations Championship, but was also a member of the ABE club. Anybody But England.

I refrained from referring to his other outing to see the supporters off on the ferry to Scotland and his forgetting to get off the boat, but I've told you that story already. Instead I said, "Fingal, I think we were discussing the meaning of . . ."

"Chutzpah. That's right." He beamed then said, "I believe I saw a prime example." His eyes took on that dreamy look they always held when he recalled the past. "It was 1935," he said. "Ireland was playing Scotland at Lansdowne Road. Not far from where my parents lived. Back then I had three close friends. You know Sir Donald Cromie and Charlie Greer."

"I should do," I said. "They both taught me."

O'Reilly's voice softened. I detected a tinge of melancholy. "I wish you'd been able to meet the fourth musketeer, Bob Beresford from near Conlig. He was my best friend." O'Reilly shook his shaggy head. "Bloody war."

I knew better than to try to pry into his wartime experiences.

O'Reilly sighed. "But that was later. Back in the '30s Bob was a typical medical student, full of beans, loved a bit of *craic*, and had little respect for authority." O'Reilly nodded at my glass. "Another?"

"I'm fine, thanks."

"Suit yourself. One thing about watching rugby matches, us students always had a few pints before the game and it was a point of honour not to miss the kick-off which was always at two-thirty in those days. We drank in Davy Byrne's pub on Duke Street. Timing was everything. You could walk it from there to the rugby pitch in half an hour. So that meant leaving the pub at five to two."

I really was trying to pay attention, but what in the name of the wee man had any of this to do with a definition or an example of chutzpah?

"Now," said O'Reilly. "I am coming to the point. . . ."

Regular readers will know that Kinky Kincaid has the sight, and sometimes I wondered about O'Reilly. He had, it seemed, just read my mind.

"Byrne's was, as a contempoary jazz musician would have said, jumping. Wall-to-wall people and the *craic* was ninety. Suddenly Charlie Greer says, 'Holy Moses. It's ten past two. We're going to miss the kick-off.' He and Cromie and I leapt to our feet. 'Come on, Bob.' You'd have thought Bob Beresford was Drake at Plymouth Ho in 1588 finishing his game of bowls before sailing off to the fight the Spanish Armada. 'Take your time,' says he. 'We've pints to finish, my car's outside, and it's only a seven-minute drive. We'll be there in no time.'"

"But," I said, "was it easier to get parking back then? When Jack Mills and I drove down we had to walk for miles after we'd left the car."

"Same in the thirties. My immediate thought was that we could park in my parents' drive but Bob would hear nothing of it. 'Just leave it to me.' We all piled into his car at quarter past two. The traffic wasn't bad on the main road, but it was slow going getting along Lansdowne through the throng of spectators heading for the turnstiles. Just outside them, Bob stops the car and says, 'Everyone out,' and proceeds to get out himself, even leaving the engine running."

My eyes must have widened. "Sounds daft to me," I said.

"Seemed daft to us too," said O'Reilly, "but we assumed Bob knew what he was doing. Between the jigs and the reels of it we got out, saw the kick-off, watched the match, and returned. No car."

"You do surprise me, Fingal," I said.

"Not as much as Bob surprised us. 'Come on,' says he and we followed as he marched straight to the nearest *Garda Síochána* station and up to the desk."

"To report a stolen car, no doubt."

"Exactly," said O'Reilly, "but the result wasn't what we expected."

"Go on."

"Bob describes the make and number plates to a big sergeant behind a desk. Your man's face, which had looked like a heiffer looking over a hedge, splits into a great grin. 'Hold the lights,' he says. 'Hold the feckin' lights. This is your lucky day, sir. We have a motor car exactly matching that description in the station car park round the back. Some buck eejit must have wanted a ride to the game. It was reported about an hour and half ago on Lansdowne Road, unoccupied and with its engine running. A constable brought it back here."

"Talk about luck," I said.

"No," said O'Reilly, "we were talking about chutzpah. I think I've made my point."

It wasn't until I'd stopped laughing that he said, "Bob had some paperwork to do, then we collected, the motor and headed back to Davy Byrne's. We had to celebrate, you see . . ."

"Your friend Bob's chutzpah?"

O'Reilly shook his head, "Nah," he said, "although it was fun. The big thing was that Ireland had beaten Scotland, twelve to five."

Cakes

AND

Biscuits

Cheese Straws

Makes 16
½ package frozen puff pastry, about 8 oz/227 g thawed
Mustard, preferably Dijon
7 oz/200 g strong cheddar cheese or Parmesan cheese, grated
1 egg, beaten

Preheat the oven to 375°F/190°C. Roll out the pastry to make an 6 by 8-inch/15 by 20-cm rectangle and spread half with mustard. Sprinkle the cheese over the mustard half and bring the other half of the pastry over the cheese. Now seal with the rolling pin and roll out again to about 6 inches/15 cm. Cut into 16 to 20 strips about 6 inches /15cm in length and twist at each end. Place on a baking sheet lined with cooking parchment and refrigerate for about half an hour, then brush with egg and bake for about 10 minutes until puffy and golden.

Dark Guinness Cake
with Jameson Cream Icing

Serves 12 or more

9 oz/265 ml Guinness

8 oz/227 g unsalted butter

14 oz/400 g superfine sugar

3 oz/85 g unsweetened cocoa powder

4½ oz/127 g sour cream

2 eggs

1 Tbsp vanilla extract

10 oz/284 g all-purpose flour

2½ tsp baking soda

Cream Topping (recipe follows)

Preheat the oven to 350°F/180°C. Line a 9-inch/23-cm springform pan with parchment paper and grease and flour it.

Pour the Guinness into a large saucepan, add the butter, and melt gently. Now remove the pan from the heat and whisk in the sugar and cocoa. Beat the sour cream, eggs, and vanilla together and pour into the batter. Finally, sift the flour and baking soda and whisk them in, then pour the batter into the baking tin. Bake for about 40 minutes, until risen and springy to the touch. Allow the cake to cool in the tin for a few minutes, then turn out onto a wire rack to cool completely. Now decorate the cake by spreading the cream topping over it so it looks like a properly poured pint of Guinness with a great head on it.

Cream Topping

    8 oz/227 g cream cheese, softened

    4 oz/113 g confectioners' sugar

    4½ oz/135 ml whipping cream

    1 Tbsp Jameson's whiskey or extra-strong black coffee

Using an electric mixer, beat the cream cheese and sugar together. Then beat in the cream and, if you are like himself, a little John Jameson Irish whiskey. My friend Flo Bishop, the councillor's wife, tells me it's very good made with a good shot of Bailey's Irish Cream.

    Now all you have to do is decorate the cake so it looks like a properly poured pint of Guinness with a great head on it. This is quite a large cake and a little goes a long way, so it would serve about 12 people.

VARIATION

Dark Guinness Layer Cake. This is a variation of the preceding recipe and will make two large loaves. It is great for a party and can be prepared well in advance.

Preheat the oven and make the batter as above. Grease two 9 by 5-inch/23 by 12-cm loaf tins, line them with parchment paper, and grease the parchment.

    Divide the cake batter into the loaf tins and bake for about 35 minutes. Allow to cool slightly, then lift from the tins by grasping the parchment and set on a wire rack to cool completely. Make the Cream Topping recipe using about 2 ounces/60 ml extra cream, so it will be a little less stiff than needed for the Guinness cake above. Remove the parchment from the loaves and slice each loaf horizontally into three layers. Re-line the tins with fresh parchment or tin foil and proceed to layer the cake and the cream topping in the tins, finishing with a layer of cream topping. Place in the refrigerator to firm up slightly. Remove from the tins, decorate with grated chocolate, and cut in slices to serve.

Ginger Biscuits

Makes About 24

3 oz/85 g all-purpose flour

3 oz/85 g old-fashioned rolled oats

2½ oz/70 g sugar

1 (2-in/5-cm) piece fresh ginger, peeled and finely chopped or grated

1 tsp ground ginger

½ tsp baking soda

4 oz/113 g butter

1 Tbsp maple syrup or golden syrup

1 Tbsp milk

Preheat the oven to 300°F/150°C. Line two baking sheets with parchment paper.

Combine the flour, oats, sugar, fresh ginger, ground ginger, and baking soda in a large bowl and mix well. Melt the butter, syrup, and milk in a saucepan and mix into the dry ingredients. Pop the dough into the fridge for about 5 minutes, until it has firmed up and cooled.

Now put heaped teaspoons of dough on the baking sheets spaced well apart, as they spread while baking. Flatten the top of each biscuit with the back of a spoon and bake 10 to 20 minutes, until lightly browned. Allow them to cool on the baking sheets; otherwise they would disintegrate. When they are cool enough to move, transfer to a wire rack. Store in an airtight container.

Guinness Gingerbread

Makes 1 cake

10½ oz/298 g all-purpose flour

1 Tbsp ground ginger

1 tsp pumpkin pie spice or Chinese five-spice powder

1 tsp ground cinnamon

1½ tsp baking powder

½ tsp baking soda

½ tsp salt

8 oz/227 g butter, softened

8 oz/227 g brown sugar

2 eggs plus 1 egg yolk

9 oz/265 ml molasses or treacle

6 oz/180 ml Guinness, flat

Preheat the oven to 350°F/180°C. Grease and flour a 9 by 5-in/23 by 12-cm loaf tin.

Sift the flour, ginger, pumpkin pie spice, cinnamon, baking powder, baking soda, and salt together into a large bowl. In a separate bowl, using an electric mixer, beat the butter and sugar together until fluffy. Add the eggs and yolk, and then the molasses and continue to beat until well mixed. Gradually add the flour mixture alternating with the Guinness; do not overbeat.

Pour the batter into the prepared tin and bake for 50 minutes to an hour, until well risen and firm to the touch.

Allow the cake to cool in the tin for a few minutes, then turn out onto a wire rack to cool completely, covered with a damp tea towel. Now you can of course eat it right away, and it really does make a nice dessert served with cream or ice cream. However, if you wrap the gingerbread in parchment and leave it in an airtight tin for a day or two, it will become more moist and delicious. Some people enjoy this with butter.

Kinky's Note:

If you find that your brown sugar has gone hard and you need to use it immediately just put it in a microwave-safe container with a piece of damp paper towel and a lid. Then microwave it on high for about 30 seconds and test it for softness. If it is still hard just give it another 30 seconds. To soften brown sugar that you do not need to use right away just put it in an airtight container, add a piece of well-moistened paper towel, cover, and leave it until the sugar absorbs the moisture. Then remove the paper and replace the lid.

Orange Sponge Cake

This is a very easy and quick-to-make cake using the "all in one" method.

Makes 1 Sandwich Cake

CAKE

6 oz/170 g butter, softened

6 oz/170 g sugar

3 eggs, at room temperature

Grated zest of 1 orange, plus juice of ½ orange

6 oz/170 g self-rising flour

1 tsp baking powder

ICING

9 oz/255 g mascarpone cheese

2 oz/56 g butter, softened

6 oz/170 g confectioners' sugar

Finely grated zest of 1 orange

FOR THE CAKE:

Preheat the oven to 325°F/170°C. Grease and flour two 8-inch/20-cm cake tins.

Using an electric mixer, beat the butter, sugar, eggs, and orange zest and juice for about a minute. Sift the flour and baking powder into a large bowl and fold this into the beaten egg and butter mixture. The mixture should now be a soft dropping consistency but if it is not, just add a little more orange juice from the unused half. Now divide the mixture between the prepared tins, smooth the tops, and bake for 30 to 35 minutes. With your finger, lightly touch the centre and if it leaves no impression and the cake springs back, they are done. Allow to cool in the tins for a shmall little minute. Gently loosen the sides of the cakes with a palette knife and ease them carefully out of the tins onto a wire rack. Allow them to cool completely.

FOR THE ICING:

Using an electric mixer, beat all the ingredients together. Place one cake on a serving plate and spread with half the icing. Place the second cake on top and spread the top and sides with the remaining icing.

Very Easy Boiled Fruit Cake

Makes 2 Cakes

1lb/455 g dried fruit (raisins, sultanas, apricots, dates, cranberries, etc.)

8 oz/227 g sugar

10 oz/295 ml warm tea

1 egg

2 Tbsp marmalade

8 oz/227 g all-purpose flour

8 oz/227 g whole-wheat flour

4 tsp baking powder

Put the fruit, sugar, and tea in a large bowl and leave to soak overnight.

The next day preheat the oven to 325°F/160°C. Grease and flour two 9 by 5-inch/23 by 12-cm baking tins. Stir the egg and marmalade into the fruit mixture, then stir in the flours and baking powder. Divide the batter between the two tins. Bake for 1½ hours, until well risen and beginning to shrink from the sides of the tin. Test by pressing gently with a finger; if done, the cake should spring back. Allow the cake to cool in the tin for a few minutes, then turn out onto a wire rack to cool completely. Serve sliced, with butter.

This cake keeps well in an airtight tin for up to four weeks, or it would, if my great friends Aggie Arbuthnot and Flo Bishop did not have such an acute sense of smell and knew when I had just baked it. Still, it's nice to sit down and have a good yarn and a cup of tea with friends.

Quick Flaky Pastry

Makes 1 Pie Case 9 inch/23 cm

6½ oz/184 g all-purpose flour

4 oz/113 g lard or margarine

½ tsp salt

A pinch of baking powder

4 tsp cider vinegar

2 oz/60 ml ice water

Chill the fat in the freezer for several hours. In a large bowl, combine the flour, salt, and baking powder. Chop the lard or grate it, using a coarse cheese grater, into the flour (or briefly process the dry ingredients and lard in a food processor). Mix the vinegar and a little water together and stir into the flour. Don't add too much water to begin with, as you can add more later, if needed. Rest the pastry, wrapped in cling film, in the refrigerator for about 1 hour. Then roll out onto a very well-floured work surface and chill in the refrigerator until needed.

Kinky's Note:

1. If you use whole-wheat flour for the rolling out, it adds a nice crunchy texture to the pastry.
2. If you are baking a blind pie shell I think it is preferable to use a metal pie tin as it gives a crisper finish than a ceramic or glass dish. You can always transfer it to a ceramic or glass dish when adding the filling.

Candy

AND

Treats

These are lovely treats and are so simple to make and sure isn't it lovely to have some in the house when children drop by? But maybe keep the truffles for the grown-ups?

Chocolate Truffles

Makes 12 to 18

12 oz/340 g good-quality dark chocolate (at least 70% cocoa), chopped

9 oz/265 ml heavy cream

4 oz/113 g unsalted butter, softened

1 Tbsp brandy

1 Tbsp unsweetened cocoa powder

Melt the chocolate in a large bowl over a saucepan containing just simmering hot water. Do not let the base of the bowl touch the water. Blend in the cream, butter, and brandy using a whisk or electric mixer. Cover and refrigerate overnight.

Sift the cocoa onto a plate. Using a teaspoon or a melon baller, scoop out balls of the mixture and roll between your palms, then in the cocoa. Place each in a paper case. If the mixture is too firm to work with just warm it up a bit. If it gets too soft, let it chill and start again. Keep the truffles in the fridge until you are ready to serve them.

Kinky's Note.

You can, of course, vary the flavour by adding ground nuts, whiskey, or vanilla extract.

Fudge

Makes about 50 squares
1 (14-oz/400-g) tin condensed milk
4 oz/120 ml milk
4 oz/113 g butter
1 tsp salt
16 oz/455 g demerara or brown sugar
2 tsp vanilla extract (optional)

Line a 7 by 11-inch/18 by 28-cm baking tin with greased parchment or grease a non-stick pan. Melt the condensed milk, ordinary milk, and butter over a low heat in the biggest heavy-bottomed saucepan you can find. Add the salt, then gradually add the sugar, stirring until the sugar has dissolved. Then turn the heat up high and watch that the mixture does not boil over. Continue to boil for 10 to 15 minutes, stirring often and making sure that the bottom of the mixture is not burning. The colour will change from a creamy white to a shade of light brown and the temperature will register about 240°F / 116°C. A drop of the mixture dropped into icy cold water will form a soft ball of fudge.

Using an electric mixer in a bowl, beat the fudge with the vanilla for about 5 minutes and pour into the baking tin. Allow to cool until almost but not quite set and mark into squares with a sharp knife. When cold, cut into squares and store in an airtight container.

Peppermint Creams

Makes about 12
1 egg white
8 oz/227 g confectioners' sugar
3 or 4 drops peppermint extract
Green food colouring (optional)

Beat the egg white in a bowl and sift in the sugar (through a sieve). Add the peppermint extract, the food colouring (if using) and mix into a paste. Taste to check for flavour and add more peppermint if necessary. Sprinkle some confectioners' sugar on the kitchen worktop. Knead the paste on the worktop. Then sprinkle more confectioners' sugar on the rolling pin and roll out flat to about ¼ inch/0.5 cm thick.

Using a tiny round or star-shaped cutter, cut out the peppermint creams and place on a plate covered with parchment paper. Then cover with a clean tea towel and leave in the fridge for an hour or so. You could store them in an airtight box—but they are so delicious they will soon disappear.

Yellow Man

This is a brittle honeycombed hard toffee sweet made famous by the ballad "The Ould Lamas Fair at Ballycastle."

CHORUS

At the ould Lammas Fair boys were you ever there
Were you ever at the Fair in Ballycastle-O?
Did you treat your Mary Ann to some Dulse and Yellow Man
At the ould Lammas Fair in Ballycastle-O?

The Lammas Fair has been held for some 400 years in Ballycastle, County Antrim, in the North of Northern Ireland on the last Monday and Tuesday in August. The Fair marks the end of summer and the beginning of the harvest and is visited each year by thousands of visitors. Live sheep and goats, hens and chickens, and traditional music give it a carnival atmosphere. As well as some 400 stalls of farm produce and crafts, there are local specialities such as dulse (a dried edible seaweed often served free in public houses to give the patrons "a thirst") and Yellow Man (a very hard honeycomb toffee suitable for teeth extraction).

Makes about 40 pieces
18 oz/500 g corn syrup or golden syrup
9 oz/255 g brown sugar
2 Tbsp vinegar
2 Tbsp water
1½ Tbsp butter
2 Tbsp baking soda

Grease a 7 by 11-in/18 by 28-cm Swiss roll pan and set aside. Very slowly heat everything except the baking soda in a heavy-bottomed saucepan but do not stir. Boil until the temperature reaches 240°F/190°C. You can test a drop on a cold plate or in water to see if it will harden. Gently stir in the baking soda; the mixture will immediately foam up. Using an electric mixer, beat for a couple of minutes and pour into the pan. Allow to cool and break into pieces with a hammer. Store in an airtight tin.

Christmas Dreams

For once I'm going to tell you a story that does not concern my senior partner, Doctor Fingal Flahertie O'Reilly. This one's about a little boy, a little girl, a chimney sweep, and Christmas dreams.

It was the day before Christmas Eve. I had been making a home visit to the Browns because Lenny had put his back out. Bed rest and aspirins would see him right. Connie had offered me a cup of tea and a biscuit and as it was my last call I had accepted. Biscuits today, but after midnight mass on Christmas Eve tomorrow we'd be going back to Number One Main Street for eggnog and slices of Kinky's Christmas cake.

We were sitting in the lounge chatting and watching young Colin Brown playing with his white mouse, Snowball, and his cousin from Larne, seven-year-old Nancy Grierson.

She was a pretty child. She had her long blonde hair tied up with green ribbons in two bunches that hung from the sides of her head. Her cornflower-blue eyes were set in an oval face and smiled out past a button nose.

Someone knocked at the front door.

"That'll be Mister Gilligan, the chimney sweep. I'll go and let him in," Connie rose, "but sit where you are, Doctor. Finish your tea."

Colin said, "I think it would be wheeker to be a sweep."

"Why?" I asked.

"Because they can get as dirty as they like and nobody minds. My mammy's always going on about washing behind my ears or telling me, 'there's enough muck on the back of your neck to make a lazy bed and grow potatoes, Colin Brown, so there is.'"

"And I'd still tell you to wash it if you were one," Connie said.

Mister Gilligan came in and greeted me and said, "Don't mind me, Doc. I'll just get on with my job." He started spreading a big canvas sheet like a second carpet in front of the living room fireplace.

Connie said, "We had ferocious blow-downs last night. Lenny said there was too much soot in the flue and it could catch fire and set the whole house alight. So it had to be swept. It's not been done for a couple of years."

"Two-and-a-half," said Mister Gilligan, "since I done the job. It needed doing then and it needs doing now." He knelt and began attaching a special wide piece of cloth to the front of the grate. It had a hole in the centre through which protruded a bamboo pole with a brass screw fitting. The brush head was on the far side of the cloth and already in the flue.

"It's a good thing Mister Gilligan came, isn't it, Colin?" Nancy said.

"Why?"

"Because it's Christmas Eve tomorrow and Santa's coming." She smiled up at him. "And you'll want to send your letter to Santa tomorrow evening when your Daddy lights the fire. I'm going to ask Santa for a doll's pram and a skipping rope when I get home to Larne."

I smiled and remembered my own childhood. You wrote the letter asking for your heart's desires, then put the missive on the fire. Even after it had burned you could still make out the words as the charred paper whirled up the chimney and straight to the North Pole. Miraculously on Christmas morning much of what you had asked for had appeared in your bedroom or under the tree.

"Aye," said Mister Gilligan, "and your Daddy, Colin, can't light a fire until I've done my job." He screwed another bamboo rod into the fitting on its predecessor and pushed. Another bamboo rod. Another push.

I was aware of a smell of soot.

Colin said, "Never mind my letter not getting to Santa. How do you think he'd like to come down a chimney that's clogged with soot?"

"Oooh," Nancy said and her eyes widened. "He'd get all dirty."

"I think," said Colin, with all the weight of his eleven years, "I think he comes in through the front door. I don't see how he could get Donner and Blitzen and all the other reindeer, them all harnessed with their jingle bells, and his sleigh up on our wee roof."

"Do you not?" asked Mister Gilligan. "Now there's a thing."

Colin was going to argue and say that it would be much easier for a man with Santa's big tummy to come in through the door. He'd never fit through the flue. Then he saw Nancy looking puzzled. He kept his mouth shut.

She frowned and said, "Daddy says he comes down the chimney. That's why we leave him eggnog and biscuits and carrots for his reindeer. We put them in the hearth and they're always gone in the morning. He does come down the flue. So there."

"You're likely right," said Colin. I could tell that he was not convinced. He turned to the sweep. "Are you nearly finished?"

Mister Gilligan screwed in one more rod. "Aye. Just about, but I'm going to need your help."

"Wheeker," Colin said. "Can I push on the rods like you?"

Mister Gilligan laughed. "That's not what I need help with."

Colin sighed.

The sweep stood up. "Come on outside, the pair of you." He headed for the door and Colin, holding Nancy's hand, followed. "Get your coats and hats and gloves," Mister Gilligan said.

Colin helped Nancy into hers, then put on his own.

I rose and said, "I'll be running along too, Connie. Thanks for the tea and don't worry about Lenny. I'll pop in tomorrow to see him."

"Thank you, Doctor." She followed me to the front door.

Outside in the garden, although the sun shone down from an enamel-blue sky, even at two in the afternoon there was still a heavy rime of frost sparkling on the little lawn. The ice on a puddle in the path crackled when I trod on it.

Across the Shore Road and past the sea wall the wind chivvied the waves of Belfast Lough like a sheep dog chases the sheep. The rollers turned to foam as they rushed up the shallowing shore. The breakers rolled the pebbles on the shingly beach, making a noise like a thousand kettle drums.

It was nippy enough out here, but I stopped to watch the final act.

Colin glanced at Nancy. Already her nose had turned red. "Right," said Mister Gilligan. "First of all I have to go up on the roof." He pointed to the chimney pots. "That one there is the pot for the living room. That wire netting has to come off, because the brush has to get out."

"I see," Colin said, staring at a conical wire-mesh contraption sitting on top of the chimney pot. "Daddy says it's to stop jack-daws nesting in the chimney."

"That's right. So I'm going to nip up my ladder, take the wire off, then I'm going back inside. Your job . . . both of you . . . is to watch until my brush pops out of the chimney, then run back in and tell me."

"We'll do that, won't we, Nancy?"

She smiled and nodded.

The sweep turned, then half-turned back. "Just one wee thing, Colin."

"What?"

"Are you quite sure Santa can't get his reindeer on your roof?"

"I . . . That wee roof? Eight big reindeer? No way." He glanced at Nancy, who was listening to every word and frowning. Her lower lip trembled. He sighed. ". . . I don't know," he said.

That, I thought, was considerate of the lad.

Mister Gilligan smiled. "I'll only be a couple of ticks." He went up the ladder rung by rung.

I watched the sweep cross the neat yellow thatch, unlatch the bird-preventer, swing it over to one side, then head back to his ladder.

"I think he's awfully brave going up there," Nancy said. "I'd be scared."

"I'd not," Colin said.

She squeezed his hand. "You're brave too, Colin and you're older than me." She looked deeply into his eyes. "I just took a quare good look at those chimney pots." She swallowed and when next she spoke I heard a catch in her voice. "They're awfully wee. Maybe you're right. Maybe Santa does come in through the front door."

I sensed tears were not far away, a cherished dream about to be shattered, and didn't know what to say.

"Excuse me," Mister Gilligan, who had clambered down, said. "Were you two arguing about whether or not Santa comes down the chimney?"

"Not really arguing," Nancy said sadly. "I think Colin's right." She sighed.

"Indeed?" said Mister Gilligan. "Well I found something at the chimney."

Colin frowned.

"I think you should have them, Nancy."

He held out his fist, knuckles down, and slowly, slowly uncurled his fingers until, when his hand was completely unclenched, there in the palm of his hand lay two silver sleigh bells.

"Now I wonder," said he, "who left these behind, and whoever it was what do you think they were doing up there in the first place?"

And Colin smiled, and Nancy laughed, and her dream was restored in all its glory. Merry Christmas. Peace on Earth. Goodwill to all.

ULSTER CHRISTMAS RECIPES

Och, Christmas, isn't it a grand time? And here in Ireland we do have our own traditions. We always keep a lighted candle in the window on Christmas Eve in case Joseph and Mary are looking for a place to stay. I clean Number One from top to bottom so if they do come they'll know they're in a well-kept house, so. The candle should be lit by the youngest member of the family and only extinguished by a girl called Mary. Willie Dunleavy, the publican's daughter of that name, is kept busy on Christmas Day. And after supper on Christmas Eve the table is set with a loaf of bread filled with caraway seeds and raisins and a jug of milk, and a large candle is lit. The front door is not locked so Joseph and Mary or indeed any traveller in need would be welcome. And while the Germans might have introduced the Christmas tree, us Irish were the first to hang a holly wreath on the front door. And there it and the house decorations stayed until Little Christmas, January the sixth. You'd have bad cess if you took them down sooner.

And one other thing. There's a joke about the Irishman

asking the priest on Christmas Eve, "Father, what time's midnight mass?" It's not as daft as it sounds. Most churches now have the Christmas Eve services much earlier these days.

And if you wish to wish a *Gaeilgeior*, an Irish speaker, merry Christmas just say *Nollaig shona duit* (null-ig hun-a dit). And that's my wish for you and I hope you are going to enjoy these Christmas recipes

Turkey with Stuffing and Gravy

To make the gravy that accompanies this turkey, you will need to first use the giblets, heart and gizzard, and wingtips to make a stock. This is best done the day before the turkey is roasted.

Serves 6 to 8

1 (10–12 lbs/4½ to 5½ kg) turkey, giblets and wingtips removed and used for Gravy (page 332)

1 oz/28 g butter, plus extra to rub over the breast

1 onion, finely chopped

8 oz/227 fresh white bread crumbs

3 Tbsp chopped fresh parsley

3 Tbsp chopped fresh thyme

Salt and freshly ground black pepper

1 egg, beaten

1 apple, peeled

Sea salt

Remove the turkey from the refrigerator about an hour before you are going to cook it to bring it to room temperature. Wash the turkey under cold running water and pat dry, inside and out. Preheat the oven to 400°F/200°C.

Melt the butter in a small frying pan over a medium heat, add the onion, and cook until soft and translucent. Mix with the bread crumbs, parsley, and thyme and season with salt and pepper. Now add the beaten egg to bind.

Carefully pull back the breast skin so that you can slide your hand into the space and put a layer of stuffing over the breast. Bring the skin back over the top and secure it with a couple of skewers. Place any remaining stuffing in the centre cavity with the apple.

Rub a little softened butter over the skin and sprinkle with sea salt. Now weigh the turkey complete with stuffing so that you can calculate the cooking time.

Place the turkey in a roasting tin, cover with foil, and cook for 20 minutes. Turn the oven down to 350°F/180°C and continue cooking at this temperature for 15 minutes per 1 lb/455 g of total turkey weight. After about 30 minutes, lift the foil and baste the turkey with the juices. Do this once or twice more, being careful not to let the oven cool down too much. Finally, when about 45 minutes of time remains, take the turkey from the oven, remove the foil, and turn the turkey breast-side down to finish cooking. To test that the turkey is ready, insert a skewer or knife into the thickest part of the bird between the leg and the breast, and if the juices run clear and there is no trace of pink then the turkey is ready. Remove to a carving dish, cover with clean tea towels, and leave to rest while you finish the gravy. Serve with the Cranberry Sauce (page 241).

Gravy
It is best to make the stock for this gravy at least a day before you cook the turkey.

Serves 6 to 8
Turkey giblets and wingtips
1 onion
1 carrot
2 celery stalks
Salt and freshly ground black pepper
2 Tbsp chopped fresh thyme
2 Tbsp chopped fresh parsley

2 Tbsp all-purpose flour
1 Tbsp butter, melted

Place the turkey giblets and wingtips in a large saucepan with the onion, carrot, and celery. Add the herbs, salt, and pepper and cover with about 4 pints/2 L of cold water. Bring to the boil and simmer for 2 or 3 hours. Strain and refrigerate until needed. When cold, remove the fat from the stock.

After the roasted turkey has been transferred to a carving dish, pour off the fat from the roasting tin. Set the roasting tin over a medium heat and deglaze it by gradually adding the stock, stirring to loosen the browned bits in the tin. Bring to the boil, stirring all the time. Strain into a saucepan. Mix the flour with the melted butter and whisk into the gravy. Cook, stirring, until thickened and season with salt and pepper to taste.

Glazed Roast Ham

Be sure you buy an uncooked, cured ham, sometimes called a "cook-before-eating" ham. You may need to check with your butcher and order ahead.

Serves 8 to 10

HAM

1 (7–10-lb/3.2 to 4.5-kg) cured uncooked bone-in ham

13 oz/385 ml Guinness

1 onion, quartered

1 Tbsp whole black peppercorns

1 bunch fresh thyme tied with string

3 bay leaves

GLAZE

3½ oz/105 ml Guinness

3 Tbsp whole-grain mustard

3 Tbsp clear honey

2 Tbsp dark brown sugar

A few whole cloves (optional)

FOR THE HAM:

Put a trivet in the bottom of a pot big enough to hold the ham. This will stop the ham from burning on the hot base of the pot. Place the ham on the trivet and pour the Guinness over it. Add the onion, peppercorns, thyme, bay leaves, and enough water to cover the ham. Cover the pot, bring to the boil, and simmer for 30 minutes per 1 pound/455 g of ham, periodically skimming off the surface scum. Add more water if necessary to keep the ham covered.

At the end of the calculated cooking time, turn off the heat and allow the ham to cool in the cooking liquid for at least 30 minutes, or until it's cool enough to handle. Then transfer the ham to a board and pat dry with paper towels. Using a small sharp knife, cut off the string, then carefully peel away and discard the skin, leaving a layer of fat exposed. Preheat the oven to 450°F/220°C.

FOR THE GLAZE:

Stir the Guinness, mustard, honey, and sugar together in a small saucepan over a gentle heat until the sugar has dissolved.

Score the fat into a diamond pattern. Insert cloves (if using) into the diamonds. Transfer to a roasting tin and, using a pastry brush, paint with the glaze. Roast the ham for 25 to 30 minutes, basting frequently with the glaze. Remove from the oven, cover with foil, and let rest for some 30 minutes. Carve and serve.

Kinky's Note:

In Ireland, "gammon" refers to raw ham, while "ham" refers to ready to eat. Gammon has been cured in the same way as bacon, whereas ham has been dry-cured or cooked. Once you've cooked your gammon, you can call it ham.

Very Easy Bread Sauce

Serves 4

1 onion, peeled

5 whole cloves

20 oz/590 ml milk

2 bay leaves

5 whole black peppercorns

4 oz/113 g fresh white bread crumbs

1½ oz/42 g butter

Salt and freshly ground black pepper

Stud the onion with the cloves and place in a saucepan with the milk, bay leaves, and peppercorns. Bring to the boil, then remove from the heat and let infuse for 15 to 20 minutes.

Discard the onion, bay leaves, and peppercorns and stir in the bread crumbs. Cook this very gently over a low heat for about 5 minutes, stirring now and again until the sauce has thickened and the bread crumbs have been incorporated. Stir in the butter and season with salt and freshly ground black pepper.

Kinky's Note:

Cloves are very strong-tasting so you really don't want to eat them. However, by studding the onion like this you just add the flavour. Lots of it.

Sweet Mince

This recipe is a traditional Irish filling for individual mince pies, served warm at Christmas. It has been used in my family down through the ages, although it would originally have contained meat. Now the only meat present is in the suet.

Makes 2 16-oz/450-g jars
8 oz/227 g suet
8 oz/227g tart apples, peeled, cored, and finely chopped
8 oz/227 g raisins
8 oz/227 g currants
6 oz/170 g demerara or brown sugar
4 oz/113 g candied peel, chopped
Grated zest and juice of 1 orange
2 oz/60 ml brandy
1 tsp pumpkin pie spice

Sterilise two 16-oz/450-g jars. Mix all the ingredients together in a large bowl. Pack into the jars and seal. Store in a cool, dark place until you want to use it.

Kinky's Note:
My recipe uses Bramley apples but if you cannot find these you could use just about any apples that you like.

Brandy Butter

Instead of brandy sauce, here's another wee Christmas speciality of mine I want to tell you about which goes down a right treat with your mince pies or Christmas pudding and it's made in no time at all.

Serves 6 to 8
4 oz/113 g unsalted butter, softened
4 oz/113 g confectioners' sugar
3 Tbsp brandy
2 Tbsp boiling water

Cream together the butter and sugar. Beat in the brandy and water until smooth. Chill until needed and serve with hot mince pies or Christmas pudding.

Christmas Cake
with Royal Icing and Marzipan

Serves 20

8 oz/227 g butter

8 oz/227 g brown sugar

4 eggs

8 oz/227 g all-purpose flour

2 oz/56 g ground almonds

1 tsp pumpkin pie spice

½ tsp cinnamon

½ tsp salt

8 oz/227 g raisins

8 oz/227 g muscatel raisins

8 oz/227 g sultanas

8 oz/227 g currants

4 oz/113 g glacé cherries

4 oz/113 g mixed peel

Grated zest of 1 orange

Grated zest of 1 lemon

Confectioners' sugar

Marzipan (recipe follows)

2 Tbsp apricot jam

Royal Icing (recipe follows)

Preheat the oven to 275°F/140°C. Grease an 8-inch/20-cm cake tin and line with parchment paper so that the paper extends above the sides by 1 inch/2.5 cm.

Using an electric mixer, cream together the butter and sugar until light and fluffy.

Add the eggs one at a time, beating in well. Stir in the flour, almonds, pumpkin pie spice, cinnamon, and salt. Finally add the raisins, currants, cherries, mixed peel, and zests. Pour the mixture into the prepared tin. Bake for 3 hours. Check for readiness by inserting a thin skewer. When it comes out clean, the cake is done. Allow the cake to cool in the tin for a few minutes, then turn out onto a wire rack to cool completely. Store in an airtight container until you are ready to ice it.

Place the Christmas cake on a cake plate or foil board. Dust your hands and work surface with a little confectioners' sugar and knead the marzipan until soft. Roll out half of it to fit the top of the cake and the rest to fit round the sides.

Warm the apricot jam, then brush the cake with the jam and place the marzipan on top. Cover with a tea towel and leave for a day or two. Spread the royal icing over the top and sides of the cake.

Kinky's Note:

You can buy marzipan and royal icing or make your own. But whichever you do, please make sure that you leave the cake for a few days after you put the marzipan on it, so the marzipan will dry out before you go putting on the royal icing, or you'll spoil it, so.

Marzipan

Makes enough to cover an 8-in/20-cm cake
5½ oz/156 g ground almonds
5 oz/142 g superfine sugar

Juice of ½ lemon
10 drops glycerine
Almond extract or vanilla extract

Mix the ground almonds and sugar together. Gradually add the lemon juice and glycerine until you get a marzipan texture. Flavor with almond or vanilla extract to taste.

Royal Icing

Makes enough to cover an 8–in/20–cm cake
3 egg whites
1 lb 5 oz/595 g confectioners' sugar, sifted
1 Tbsp lemon juice
1½ tsp glycerine (optional)

Using an electric mixer, lightly whisk the egg whites, adding the sugar at intervals. Beat well until the icing reaches soft peaks. Add the lemon juice and the glycerine (if using).

Christmas Pudding

Plan to make this pudding six to twelve months before you eat it. It matures and tastes much better, and is moister, too.

> *Makes 1 large (52-oz/1½-litre) pudding or 2 small (28-oz/¾-litre) puddings*
> 6 oz/170 g fresh bread crumbs
> 13½ oz/405 ml milk
> 10½ oz/298 g sugar
> 9 oz/255 g suet
> 9 oz/255 g currants
> 9 oz/255 g raisins
> 6 oz/170 g grated carrot
> 6 oz/170 g mashed potato
> 6 oz/170 g all-purpose flour
> 3 oz/85 g mixed peel
> 1½ tsp ground nutmeg
> ½ tsp salt
> 3 eggs, beaten
> 4 tsp molasses or treacle

Grease one large (52-oz/1½-litre) or two small (28-oz/¾-litre) bowls. Put the crumbs in a very large bowl. Heat the milk to the boiling point and pour it over the crumbs. Add the sugar and leave to soak for 30 minutes. Mix in the suet, currants, raisins, carrot, mashed potato, flour, mixed peel, nutmeg, and salt, mixing very well. Finally, add the eggs and molasses and beat very well. Put the mixture into greased bowls, cover, and place over a trivet or upturned saucer in a lidded saucepan of boiling water and steam for 4 hours. Continue to add boiling water from time to time to ensure that the saucepan does not boil dry. Store in a cool place wrapped in parchment paper in an air-tight tin.

Then on Christmas day steam for a further 2 hours. Turn out and garnish with a sprig of holly and serve with Brandy Sauce (page 246).

Kinky's Note:

You can use special bowls with their own lids or else cover the bowl with aluminium foil. I use parchment paper, then brown paper and tie it on with string, making a handle with the string. If you haven't got a doctor handy you do need to be very careful with the boiling water, so. This method of cooking by setting the pudding inside another container of boiling water is often referred to as a bain-marie.

Irish Coffee

A lot of Doctor O'Reilly's friends enjoy an Irish coffee; that's why I'm giving you the recipe, but himself can be a purist in some things. I thought he was going to take the rickets once when an American guest asked for Coca-Cola in his Jameson. "Kinky," says the doctor after the guest had gone, "only a heathen would do that to a good whiskey. There's only two ways to drink it, neat or hot." So I'll not be serving him Irish coffee.

Makes 1 coffee
4 oz/120 ml strong black coffee, hot
1 large measure (2 oz/56 g) Jameson's Irish whiskey
1 Tbsp heavy cream, lightly whipped
Sugar (optional)

Warm a stemmed glass with hot water and discard the water. Pour the coffee into the glass, add sugar if using and then the whiskey. Pour the cream over a hot teaspoon to float on top of the coffee. Serve with Chocolate Truffles (page 311).

A Hot Irish

Whilst Doctor O'Reilly wouldn't adulterate his precious John Jameson with anything at all, it was a different matter when he needed a wee hot one. You see, a hot whiskey is a well-known traditional "cure-all" for the winter sniffles. It was said that if it didn't cure you, sure you didn't mind because you felt all the better for having it anyway. It's also considered to be a delicious digestive or a nightcap before bed.

Makes 1 "wee one"
Boiling water
Good Irish whiskey (Jameson or Powers is ideal)
2 tsp sugar
7 or 8 whole cloves
1 lemon slice

Put a teaspoon into a stemmed heatproof glass and pour boiling water into the glass to warm it. Discard the water and pour a measure of whiskey (any size) into the warmed glass. Just leave enough room to add an equal quantity of boiling water, then add the sugar, cloves, and a good slice of lemon. Stir until the sugar has dissolved and drink while it is hot. You might need to wrap a wee napkin around the glass if it's too hot.

Epilogue

Today's Friday and, glory be, the book's nearly all done. I'll not be truly busy cooking for another half hour so I'm going to write this epilogue and at last put the manuscript to bed.

I'm sitting, pen in hand at the table in my cosy kitchen this evening at Number One Main Street, Ballybucklebo, where I've worked these many years. I have the Jerusalem artichoke soup made and ready to heat. I popped a beef Wellington into the oven five minutes ago so it'll be ready to serve when the guests have arrived, had their pre-dinner drinks, and their soup. The beef's roasting and it smells lovely. The spuds are ready for boiling so I can mash them and make champ, and the carrots peeled and ready to cook. We'll top the dinner off with sticky toffee pudding and a cheese board.

Doctor O'Reilly's got a nice white Entre-Deux-Mers chilled to have with the soup and a Châteauneuf-du-Pape to follow. He's not a great lover of sweet dessert wines, but there'll be a good Taylor's port or a Rémy-Martin XO cognac to go with the coffee. I do think his and his wife Kitty's guests—Doctor Barry Laverty and his lovely fiancée, Sue Nolan; Mister Charlie Greer the brain surgeon and Sir Donald Cromie the orthpaedic surgeon, both classmates of Doctor O'Reilly in Trinity in Dublin in the thirties; and their wives—will know they've been well fed and watered, so.

Feeding people either with formal dinners like tonight's or ordinary day-to-day meals has been a big part of my life's work, but I never thought when I set out to write this book what a labour of love it would be, so. It does please me very much to cook and to have my work appreciated. Until now the enjoyment has come from those who come here to Number One Main Street, Ballybucklebo. Folks like Doctor O'Reilly's brother Lars the solicitor, the marquis of Ballybucklebo and his sister, Myrna, Doctor Ronald Fitzpatrick from the Kinnegar, and Doctor Nonie Stevenson the new assistant, to name a few.

And now my recipes and those of friends and special contributors are going to find a wider audience. I do hope readers will have fun exploring the tastes of Ireland, many of which I learned from my ma.

And it's not for me to take the whole credit. Many of those who contributed are recognised in my acknowledgements, but I want to pay special thanks to Doctor Barry Laverty for taking the trouble to pen the stories. In truth I had very little editing to do. Dorothy

Tinman arranged the artwork and has done a wonderful job. *Go raibh milde maith agat,* thank you very much.

And I must say a shmall little word about Patrick Taylor. I never for a minute thought when he started spinning his *Irish Country Doctor* yarns that the recipes of a County Cork woman from a wee place called Béal na Bláth would ever find their way into a book of their own. But they have, praise be. And I truly hope you enjoy cooking them as much as I do.

And now I hear the first guests arriving and being greeted by himself, and that's time for me now to get on with my work, so.

Until the next time, *Slan leat agus beannacht De agat.* Farewell and God bless you.

Maureen "Kinky" Auchinlech

Some Helpful Advice from Kinky

I thought it might be useful if I put all the wee notes that I'd made here and there through the recipes in one place to make them easy to find. So here they are:

SOUP/VEGETABLES/FRUIT/SAUCE

When you are making soup, covering the vegetables with parchment paper and cooking very gently for about 10 minutes creates steam and is called "sweating." This enables the maximum amount of moisture and flavour to be extracted.

When using fresh tomatoes, immerse them in boiling water for a minute then plunge them into ice cold water and draw a line round the tomato with a sharp knife. This will make it easy to peel off the skin.

Microwaving lemon halves for 10 to 15 seconds before you squeeze them will double the yield of juice.

Melting butter and stirring an equal amount of flour into it is called making a roux (pronounced "roo") and can be the basis for many sauces. It is a good idea to make more than you need as it will keep wrapped in cling film or foil in the refrigerator. However, the rule is that if your roux is warm you whisk a cold liquid into it. If the roux is cold you whisk in warm liquid

BREAD/CAKES/DUMPLINGS/PASTRY

Flour is a little bit like a sponge and it can absorb moisture from the atmosphere. Miss Sue Nolan, the school mistress, is very learnéd in these matters and she tells me that the amount of moisture in flour can vary because of damp weather and humidity in the atmosphere. How you store flour also makes a difference. So some days you may need to add more liquid than others.

When making bread and farls if you are in a hurry you could substitute vegetable oil for butter and add with the buttermilk.

When measuring both oil and treacle (or molasses), if you use the spoon to measure the oil first, the treacle or molasses will run off the spoon more easily.

If you are using the oven or a bread-proofing oven programme to let yeast dough rise, it really gives the rising process a head start if you create steam by placing a baking tin containing boiling water in the floor of the oven.

When making dumplings on the surface of a stew, do not open the lid when cooking and keep the liquid just at a simmer and the dumplings will be light and fluffy.

The batter for Yorkshire puddings can be made in advance up to three days before you make the puddings, but bring it back to room temperature before cooking. Do not open the door while the puddings are cooking or they might collapse. Prick with a toothpick to allow the steam to escape.

When rolling out pastry use whole-wheat flour. This adds a nice crunchy texture to the pastry.

I think it is preferable to use a metal pie tin for blind-baking a pie shell, as it gives a crisper finish than a ceramic or glass dish. You can always transfer it to a ceramic or glass dish when adding the filling.

When icing a cake with marzipan, be sure to leave it for a few days after you put on the marzipan, to allow time for it to dry out, before you put on the royal icing.

Christmas pudding matures and tastes much better if you can remember to make it six months to one year before you need it.

EGGS

The secret for successful meringue is to make sure that not a single drop of egg yolk gets into the mixture and to ensure that your bowl and beaters are perfectly clean and grease-free. I rub a splash of vinegar on a paper towel round the bowl and beaters.

For perfect fried eggs, add a teaspoon of water to the frying pan, then cover and turn the heat down very low or off and the top of the eggs will cook in the steam.

Cooling hard-boiled eggs quickly under cold running water will prevent them from discolouring.

FISH

If serving fish raw, always use fish that has been frozen as this destroys any parasites that may have been present.

MEAT

When making stew, if you have time, do it on the previous day because it improves the flavour. Refrigerate overnight and it will be easier to remove any fat that has solidified on the surface. Then when you cook it the following day, you can make the suet dumplings or cobbler topping to finish it off.

The difference between cottage pie and shepherd's pie is that you use lamb instead of beef to make a shepherd's. This is very good too, and reminds me so much of my childhood and a man called Connor MacTaggart, but you'll have to read *An Irish Country Girl* to find out why.

It is easy to coat meat in flour in a plastic bag. Just put the flour and seasoning in the bag, add the meat, close the top, and give it a good shake around.

The difference between gammon and ham, simply put, is that gammon is raw and ham is ready to eat. Gammon has been cured in the same way as bacon, whereas ham has been dry-cured or cooked. Once you've cooked your gammon, you can call it ham.

EVAPORATED MILK

Evaporated milk is unsweetened and is milk which has had about 60 percent of the water removed via evaporation. Condensed milk is sweetened. Sixty percent of the water has also been removed from condensed milk, but it differs in that sugar has been added. Unsweetened condensed milk is a redundant term. It is simply evaporated milk.

SEASONED FLOUR

Seasoned flour is plain flour to which you've added salt and pepper.

SUGAR

To soften hard brown sugar that you need to use immediately, just put it in a microwave container with a piece of damp paper towel and cover with a lid. Then heat it on high for about 30 seconds and test it for softness. If it is still hard just give it another 30 seconds.

To soften brown sugar that you do not need to use right away just put it in an airtight container, add a piece of well-moistened paper towel, replace the lid, and leave it until the sugar absorbs the moisture, then remove the paper and seal it in an airtight container.

GINGER

Keep ginger in the freezer and it is easy to grate while frozen.

Acknowledgments

Without the unstinting help and encouragement of many people we could not have written and produced this book. They are:

Tom Doherty, Kristin Sevick, Cheryl Redmond, Irene Gallo, Alexis Saarela, Jamie Broadhurst, and Fleur Matthewson, all of whom have contributed enormously to the literary and technical aspects of bringing the work from rough draft to the bookshelf.

Natalia Aponte and Victoria Lea, our English rights literary agents.

Jessica and Rosie Buchman, our foreign rights agents.

Tristan Allen, Deputy General Manager, and Paul McKnight, Executive Chef, of Culloden Hotel and Spa, Holywood Co. Down N Ireland.

Gale Robinson, in Saltspring Island, British Columbia, for the use of her pottery soup bowls used in photography.

Frances Nixon, in Kincardine, Ontario, for inspiring the recipe for Guinness Cake.

Don Kalancha, Joe Maier, and Michael Tadman, who keep us right in contractual matters.

To all our friends in Channel Ridge, Saltspring Island, for their support.

To you all, we tender our most heartfelt gratitude and thanks.

Glossary

bain-marie: A baking tin or dish placed in a roasting tin or saucepan of water. It allows the food to cook indirectly and protects delicate flavours.

bake blind: To bake or part bake a pastry shell without the filling. This ensures that the shell will remain crisp. Simply prick the pastry, lightly, with a fork. Cover with parchment and add baking beans or rice to prevent the pastry rising.

baste: To moisten and flavour meat or fowl when roasting by spooning the pan juices over it or using a basting brush.

beurre manié: Equal parts of cold butter and flour blended together and whisked into simmering cooking liquid to thicken it after cooking. Different from a roux, which is cooked beforehand.

boil: To keep liquid at a temperature that produces bubbles that break the surface.

deglaze: To dissolve the residue at the bottom of the cooking pan by adding liquid such as wine or water and heating over a high temperature until the liquid boils and incorporates the remnants. This will then form the basis for a sauce or a gravy.

degrease: To remove the fat from the cooking liquid. This is usually done by skimming it from the top after the liquid has been chilled.

fold: To combine ingredients without knocking out the air. This is usually done by gently adding or folding the lighter ingredient to the heavier one in a large bowl. Run a spatula or large metal spoon round the side and across the bottom of the bowl so that you are folding the mixture over itself. Turn the bowl 90 degrees and repeat until just combined. Do not overwork.

glaze: To coat the surface of food with a sweet or savoury mixture such as honey or egg to produce a shiny surface when cooked.

gratin: A dish topped with crumbs or grated cheese and dotted with butter, and then placed under a grill until a golden crust is formed on top. It is usually served in its baking dish.

infuse: To extract maximum flavour by steeping in hot liquid.

knead: To work dough (or marzipan) with the heel of the hand in a pressing and folding motion until it becomes elastic and smooth.

liquidise: To change solid food into liquid using a blender.

marinade: A mixture of either liquid or dry ingredients to flavour and give moisture to food, which may remain in the marinade for several hours before cooking.

puree: To mash or blend food with a mixer to form a smooth, thick mixture.

poach: To cook food gently, just submerged in liquid that is just below the boiling point; see the definition of "simmer."

roux: A cooked mixture of fat, usually butter, and flour used to thicken liquids such as sauce, soup, or stew. A roux is made by melting butter, adding the flour, and then cooking the mixture for several minutes to cook off the taste of raw flour.

sauté: To fry quickly, usually in butter, in a small pan.

sear: To cook food (usually meat) over high heat so that it browns quickly and seals in the juices, after which the heat is reduced for the remaining cooking time.

score: To make shallow incisions in a cut of meat or outside layer of fat to aid penetration of heat or a marinade or just for decoration.

sift: To put fine ingredients such as flour, baking soda, etc. through a fine sieve.

simmer: To keep a liquid at just below the boiling point so the liquid just trembles.

skim: To remove scum, fat, or froth from the surface of stock or soup.

steam: To cook over boiling water in a closed container.

sweat: To cook vegetables gently over a low heat, covered with parchment paper and the pan lid, so that steam is created, and the maximum amount of moisture and flavour is extracted.

toss: To thoroughly combine several ingredients by mixing lightly.

zest: The thin outer rind (not the white pith) of lemon or orange, usually grated or cut thinly.

Index